Clas
Vo

CW00969960

BEDFORD
LIGHT
COMMERCIALS
OF THE
1950s & '60s

Alan Earnshaw
&
Robert W. Berry

Trans-Pennine Publishing

MILK · CREAM · BUTTER · EGGS

EDINBURGH & DUMFRIESSHIRE

CONTENTS

Front Cover: *In a posed publicity shot, an early MkII van epitomises the outstanding role the CA van played for almost two decades, the British builder's workhorse.*

Rear Cover Top: *The new Radiation Domestic Appliance company fleet in 1965, with five HA vans, five CA vans and three TK box vans pictured in front of the firm's earlier black-liveried MkI CA vans.*

Rear Cover Bottom: *A MkII CAL fitted with the 380 cubic feet capacity Arlington 'Crystal' Pantechnicon body and pictured working as a Vauxhall demonstrator in 1963. Note the other CA and TJ models in the background.*

Title Page: *With the magnificent backdrop of Edinburgh Castle, this view shows one of the CA vans that were so popular with roundsmen in the period. Delivering milk, eggs, butter, and cream for Edinburgh & Dumfries Dairy, it was No.1 in their fleet.*

This Page: *With a rustic background that ought to appeal to Peter Jones(who commissions those superb porcelain models), we see an M-Type belonging to the millers John Baker Ltd. at Barnham Mill in Sussex on 3rd April 1952.*

The **Nostalgia Road** Series ™
is conceived, designed and published by
Trans-Pennine Publishing Ltd.
PO Box 10
Appleby-in-Westmorland
Cumbria, CA16 6FA
Tel. 017683 51053
Fax. 017683 53558
ISDN. 017683 53684
e-mail trans.pennine@virgin.net
(A Quality Guild registered company)

Reprographics
Barnabus Design & Repro
Threemilestone, Truro
Cornwall, TR4 9AN
01872 241185

And Printed in Cumbria by
Kent Valley Colour Printers Ltd.
Shap Road Industrial Estate
Kendal, Cumbria LA9 6NZ
01539 741344

THIS BOOK IS DEDICATED TO MY WIFE LARRAINE FOR THIRTY HAPPY YEARS OF MARRIED LIFE
3RD JULY 1971 - 3RD JULY 2001

INTRODUCTION

This book is (in many ways) a journey into the youth of the authors, both of whom were born in the early 1950s and spent much of their childhood taking an interest in the cars and commercial vehicles that were to be seen in their home town of Huddersfield. Like most boys of our time, we both had a large collection of die-cast metal cars produced by toy-makers like Dinky and Corgi.

Those readers who still collect such models or can remember the days when they played with such toys, will undoubtedly recall that a large number of these models were based on the Bedford commercial vehicles built by Vauxhall Motors at Luton and Dunstable.

Yet it was the real thing that held most interest for me, and I witnessed a large variety of Bedford light commercials in the town. In fact they were so versatile and economical (both to purchase and maintain), that they were in widespread use in Britain and overseas. What is more, they were so 'common', that the company adopted the most appropriate of advertising slogans, **You See Them Everywhere!**

Indeed you did, from newspaper vans and milk floats, to builders trucks and the perennial favourite of all children - ice cream vans. But the range included much more than the light commercial, as Bedford made everything from buses and heavy trucks, to fire engines, ambulances and military vehicles. Indeed, if you were to look through the Vauxhall archives, you would be staggered by the vast array of things the company produced under the Bedford marque.

Above: *In a picture taken on 16th February 1948. we show a line up of three Bedford service vehicles employed by the North Worcestershire Garage, Stourbridge. The fleet comprises of a PC van (FUY 777), used as a general service unit), a 5-/6-cwt HC van (GAB 777, used as Bedford Trucks parts van) and a 2³/4-ton lightweight O-Type salvage/breakdown truck.*

This book reflects part of that record, and is just one of the **Nostalgia Road** range of titles that details the history of Bedford vehicles. Three books detail the history of Bedford Buses, and four books are currently being produced on the commercial vehicles. All these books have been written with the co-operation of Vauxhall Motors Ltd., and produced in close association with Vauxhall Heritage Services. In addition to these books, a series of five publications are also being produced for Vauxhall Heritage Services on the history of the Vauxhall car range

We (the authors) are therefore deeply indebted to Vauxhall for giving us this unique privilege, and making this wonderful collection of photographs available to illustrate the book. This archive material is not currently available to the general public, but by making it available for use in these publications, the company have done their utmost to place these images in the public domain for all to enjoy. In turn I hope that I have done justice to everyone's expectation in the pages that follow.

Alan Earnshaw   Appleby-in-Westmorland, July 2001

TWENTY YEARS OF PROGRESS

You See Them Everywhere, the slogan adopted by Vauxhall in 1934 to market their Bedford range of commercial vehicles was certainly proved true by the start of 1950. Yet despite the firm's dominance of the British commercial vehicle market, Bedford had only been building vans, trucks and buses for two decades. So one might ask, how did such phenomenal success come about. Others might ask how the Bedford name was derived, as even Vauxhall's own publications state that the records on this are unclear.

To answer this we need to travel back to the troubled economic times of the 1920s, and the situation facing many car manufacturers of this time. Vauxhall had begun car production back in 1903 at their factory in London, and relocated production to Luton in 1905. A successful period of production followed, and during the second half of the next decade, the works were substantially buoyed up by orders from the War Department. For example, during World War I, no less than 2,000 D-Type army staff cars were supplied. However, by the early 1920s, the shaky European economy presented a number of problems for the British automotive industry and several companies were ripe for take-over. As the American economy was still strong at that time, it is not surprising to report that the US car-making giants General Motors acquired Vauxhall in 1925.

Some four years later the same American company acquired a controlling interest in the German firm Opel, before purchasing the rest of the shares in 1931. With this involvement in European vehicle manufacture, GM began to expand their Chevrolet brand here in Britain. By the start of the 1930s a range of British-Built Chevrolets, mostly produced at Luton, were being marketed to an audience keen to purchase economically-priced commercial vehicles. Yet despite their apparent success, GM were facing something of an uphill struggle, as there was an under-current of anti-American sentiment running through certain sectors of British business due to the events following the Wall Street Crash in October 1929.

With the collapse of the US economy, Europe was thrown into financial crisis for a second time, and as a consequence there was a backlash that affected the public's view on buying American products. Whilst it was not envisaged as a long-term problem, Vauxhall had already been toying with the idea of a name for their commercial range that could be readily identified as being a British brand. Ford had already gone some way to resolving this problem, and when they moved their production facilities from Trafford Park in Manchester to Dagenham in Essex, they actively began to promote the name 'Ford of Great Britain'. Yet the best example is the Hudson Car Company who adopted the name Essex for their British-built cars, to reflect the county in which they were assembled.

Top Left: *Whilst the O-Type lorry nominally weighed in at 3-tons, and thus out of our 'light commercial' category of under 3-tons, a few lightweight models were produced in the 35-cwt//55-cwt range. Just how many were built is uncertain, but this 2³/4-tonner has a body by Hinds of Carlisle for Tweedies Motors, Dumfries.*

Top Right: *This is part of a line up of seven PC newspaper delivery vans supplied to the* Sunderland Echo *in 1951. Bedford light commercials were well-liked by many newspaper proprietors and several examples of 'paper-vans' appear in this book - I hope this will therefore prompt a few good reviews in the regional press.*

Middle Right: *With a canvas tilt cover and a sliding door in the back of the cab, this shortened 30-cwt M-Type was supplied by Barkers of Bolton to the local firm Tillotsons Newspapers Ltd. in 1949.*

Bottom Right: *At the Goyt Valley Waterworks on 12th September 1950, a PC Utilecon and a 'special' 2-ton tipper are seen in the employment of Stockport Corporation.*

By adopting a County name with which buyers in Britain (and the Dominions) could associate, a sound marketing strategy was formed. It worked well in the case of the Essex Marque, and it worked even better when emulated by Vauxhall. Choosing the name Bedford, the shire county in which the Luton works were located, was much more prosaic than British-built Chevrolet could ever be. It was quickly established in the minds of dealers, body-builders and buyers alike, as being a new British-made range of commercials despite the quite obvious American influence in both engineering and design.That little fact aside, the Bedford marque grew dramatically in the 1930s, starting out with the WHG/WLG 2-ton chassis and the WS 30-cwt chassis all introduced in 1931. Bus chassis were also introduced, but the story is told in our companion book *Bedford Buses of the 1930s & '40s*. In 1932 an 8-cwt van was derived from a car chassis in the form of the VYC/VXC, and this was later complemented by the ASYC/ASXC in 1939.

By the year 1933 a 3-ton chassis, the WTH/WTL, had arrived but it was not until 1938 that a light-weight 5/6-cwt was produced. This was the HC, which would remain in production until 1948. At the same time Bedford were testing the 10/12-cwt JC van, which would be introduced the following year and would last (as the PC) until 1952 when the famous CA was launched. The JC had replaced the 12-cwt BYC/BXC, which had run from 1934 to 1939, but it was only one of a number of important changes that were introduced on the eve of World War II.

As several of these new models lasted in production into the early 1950s (and also stayed in service until the 1960s), we will begin our account with a brief look at the models in production at the start of the two decades being considered in this book. We will begin with the K-Type and the M-Type, but as this book covers the Bedford light commercial models (under 3-ton), the most famous of all those 1939 developments the O-Type is excluded. It will, however, be covered in our forthcoming book, *Bedford Commercials Of the 1950s & '60s*.

THE K-TYPE 30- 40-CWT

Towards the end of the 1930s, the Bedford models that had been introduced earlier in the decade were by then becoming rather dated. More importantly it was also considered by the dealers that the range was inadequate at meeting the expectations of a commercial sector that was starting to boom again after the hard years of the Depression. Cheap and cheerful might have been what was needed in the early 1930s, but by 1936 something more was obviously required.

In September 1936, two design draughtsmen (one mechanical - one styling) left Luton for the General Motors plant in the USA, returning in December with a number of ideas that were to be adapted for the British market. These changes would not be introduced for well over two years, although a re-vamp of several models would take place in 1938 after a new set of uniform body pressings were designed for the cab, bonnet and radiator grill on the 20-cwt to 3-ton range of commercials. The same pressings, produced by the Willenhall Radiator Company, would also appear on the new 3- to 5-ton O Type models that would be launched in July 1939.

It is patently obvious that the new range of commercials introduced that summer was not stilted by the outbreak of war in September 1939, as many writers have suggested. If anything it was quite the contrary, as the range of K- M- and O- types were quite clearly designed to meet the needs of the forthcoming conflict. As early as 1935-6 Vauxhall-Bedford had begun working closely with the War Department in a number of areas, including a review of the light to middle-weight trucks that would be needed by the armed forces if and when war with Germany became a reality. The Luton-built models having an obvious economical appeal to the military!

The first of these new models was the K-Type, which effectively replaced the WS 30-cwt model that had been introduced in April 1932. In itself the WS was really a lighter version of the 2-ton WHG, and both models shared the same 131-inch (3.3m) wheelbase and the same 26.3hp six-cylinder petrol engine producing 64bhp. Significant improvements were made to the WS and WHG at the end of 1932, giving (primarily) an increase in load space. The advent of a 3-ton model, the WT series in November 1933, led to a facelift being applied to the WS/WHG in 1935, giving them the 'bulldog' front end of their heavier stablemate.

Top Left: *This K-Type truck has a clear indication of its model type, for on the rear tailgate is the legend KD2 meaning 2-ton dropside version. As it carries a spare wheel and tyre, the model is definitely post-1947, as up to this time the continuing rubber shortages meant that trucks left the factory with just a wheel and no spare tyre.*

Top Right: *What a line up of Bedford's in this May 1950 scene at Kinloch's wholesale grocery warehouse in Tottenham, London. It provides an interesting comparison of post-war Bedfords, showing first a K-Type 'pickle van' with Brother Bung Products, then an ex-army OWLE 5-tonner fitted with a civilian body for Crosbie's Pure Foods, and finally a new OL 4-ton van operated by the LMS Railway.*

Middle Right: *Much of the reprographic work on the Nostalgia Road series is done in Truro, so here is a picture for the team at Barnabus. It shows a 700 cubic foot pantechnicon built on a K-Type chassis by Tiverton Coachbuilders in Devon for Criddle & Smith Ltd., Truro.*

Bottom Right: *About as big as you could get on the K-Type, this pantechnicon took the overall weight above 3-tons, and really stretched the chassis beyond its capacity. Used by Paramount Transport, SMU 618 is seen here unloading textiles at Southend Airport for export to Belgium.*

The changes that customers were demanding were partially resolved in 1938 when the engine was up-rated to a 27.34hp unit producing 72bhp. But it was those 1939 changes that saw the arrival of the K-Type. In all, four models were announced, each being available in either 30-cwt or 40-cwt specification. These were the KZ, chassis or chassis cowl, the KC chassis cab, the KD dropside truck or the KV factory-built van. However, not all these models would go into full production before war broke out a few months later. Essentially production of the K-Type came to a halt in the spring of 1940, but since June 1939 no less than 9,858 chassis of the K-, M- and O- Type had been made.

Mind you, although production officially came to an end in favour of the light-weight M-Types, it is clear that several K-Types were built after 1940, but this may only have been achieved by the utilisation of existing components that had been put in to stock before the embargo on building was put into place. Several flat fronted 30-cwt forward control delivery vans, for example, were produced in 1942, and these went to the grocery merchant Beechwood in London and also to the Express Dairy Company. Ten normal control bonneted models were supplied to the London Midland & Scottish Railway in 1943, and British Dyes in Manchester obtained two K-Type chassis with Steel Barrel tanker bodies in 1944. There may well have been others, but these are just a few that can be readily identified. Naturally, the bulk of production was aimed at war-use, and even when peace was resumed, the prolific output on the M-Type models reduced demand for the K-Type. Indeed, so many war-surplus MWs came on to the market in 1945-6, that Bedford did not find it viable to launch into heavy production on the K-Type for some time.

Top Left: *Carrying dropside bodies, a pair of K-Type lorries (JHY 770-1) are seen at Avonmouth Docks in the latter part of 1954. Employed by the ship repairers J. Jefferies & Son, this pair have obviously seen hard work but the picture is included as it shows both the short wheelbase (JHY 771) and the long wheelbase model nearest the camera - but note the overhang beyond the rear axle on this truck.*

Middle Left: *Another lwb model chassis is shown with this mobile dental clinic, which operated in the far north of Scotland - I sure hope that the thing was stationary when they used the drill!*

Bottom Left: *In the absence of anywhere else to place a picture of a lightweight O-Type, we show here a 30-cwt short wheelbase chassis cab, which was supplied to York City Council by local dealer Leedham's. It carries a Lacre Road Sweeper and is working at the junction of Thanet Road.*

Quite when production fully resumed on the K-Type is not clear, as so many components were common with the M- and O- Types. Again there are indications of production continuing throughout the first post-war years, but it was not until 1948 that the K-Type began to feature heavily in Bedford publicity. When it did reappear, it was advertised as a 30cwt model, but as the 1978 Vauxhall publication *You See Them Everywhere* states:- 'the K was back to being a 30-cwt job, having shed the extra 10-cwt at some hard-to-determine point.' A major innovation on the KV from the same year was the introduction of sliding load-space doors on the side of each factory-built van.

From the slow faltering start on the postwar K-Type in 1946, the model had once again come to be in big demand by the end of the decade, and progressive improvements were introduced in the austerity years. Included in the major advances was the application of higher load ratings, the introduction of hydraulic brakes and the advent of the new 'Extra Duty Engine'. Introduced in the Spring of 1950, this new six-cylinder engine was similar to the old 28hp unit but developed up to 84bhp. Basically designed at improving performance on the O-Type models of 3-tons and above, it was nevertheless utilised on the K- and M- Types, but in a modified form that produced 76bhp.

As the accompanying pictures reveal, the K-Type was used for a variety of different purposes during the 1950s, and these ranged from municipal authority to government work, and from small one-man-businesses to large fleets. It was also a popular export model, and a great many were supplied to countries all over the world - especially to states within the British Empire. From pictures within the Vauxhall archive it is clear however, that a good many of those supplied for overseas use were given loadings well beyond their stated capacity and yet many stayed in regular use down until the 1970s and even 1980s.

The K-Type continued to play an important role in many applications until it was finally supplanted by a new range of middle-weight Bedfords in the Spring of 1953. All the pictures in this section show models built in the 1950s, and therefore these represent the final stages of development of a model that was to span no less than 15 years!

THE M-TYPE 15-CWT TO 3-TON

As stated in the previous section, June 1939 saw the arrival of the new Bedford commercial range, and included within this range was the 2- to 3-ton Bedford M-Type. Despite the many changes from the W-series Bedfords, there was still a lot about the M-Type's appearance that was reminiscent of the early 1930s models. For example the gearbox, common throughout the range of models introduced in 1939, was virtually unchanged from the model first introduced in 1931. It had a distinct GM feel about it, and the wailing sound it made was not unrecognised by American servicemen who drove these trucks during the war years. The gearbox still employed straight-toothed gears with sliding-mesh engagement on all indirect ratios. As the Chevrolet influence continued in the Bedford range, you might have thought that GM would have been quite satisfied, but rather surprising the company decided to reintroduce the Chevrolet 2- to 3-ton truck into the British market, and it opened a plant at Southampton in 1939 to handle this model as well as Opel trucks.

Top Right: *Having mentioned Carlisle in an earlier page, we do so again with a view of a 30-cwt M-Type used by the local Vauxhall-Bedford dealers SMT as an emergency service vehicle. The body on this unit was built in the company's own workshops.*

The M-Type was aimed at the 2- to 3-ton market, and therefore was ideally placed to supplant both the WL and the WT series, allowing the new O-Type to cater for the 3- to 5-ton market. However, a much lighter, stripped down version of the M-Type had already been devised, in effect making a range that would be available in 15-cwt, 20cwt, 25-cwt, 30-cwt and 2- to 3-ton capacities.

This had begun not long after the two Vauxhall designers had returned from America as, by 1937, the talk of rearmament was firmly in everyone's mind both in Luton and Detroit. In itself this was a major reason for financing a £175,000 (£9.5 million at today's prices) development project at Luton. Completed in 1938, the new 'V Block' housed around 350 engineering staff and gave unrivalled facilities for the design and development of all types of vehicle.

Top Left: *Although the M-Type was promoted as a new Bedford model there was much that could be traced back to the earlier Chevrolet trucks, especially the pressed-disc wheels with the projecting hubs. These are clearly shown in this view of a forward-control 30-cwt van in service with Henry Kingham & Sons, Watford.*

Middle Left: *The breakdown truck shown on page nine would have been supplied as a chassis/cab version, but the K-Type also came as a chassis/cowl. This was once a common sight all over Britain as it was delivered to body builders and coachworks, usually by drivers sitting on a wooden box and wearing flying helmets, bomber jackets and thick clothing. This view of the KZ model well illustrates the chassis.*

Bottom Left: *In searching out pictures for this book we found views of mobile dental surgeries, delousing vans, infestation control units and even a mobile diphtheria immunisation clinic for Hull in 1950.*

In 1935 Vauxhall had attended War Department trials in Wales, but their results at Llangollen were only partially successful. Whilst their 2-ton model had received some acclaim, it was clear that the army were looking for a 15-cwt truck. Therefore the modified WHG truck and the 12-cwt BYC van were not suited for the military's needs. The War Department specification was for a 15GS4x2 (15-cwt General Service Truck with one driving and one leading axle). There was also an emerging need for a 15GS4x4 as well, and in this regard Vauxhall held a series of meetings at Luton. Whilst military officials were pleased with what they saw on the mechanical side of things, coupled with reliability in the field and economy of purchase, the styling of the new Bedford commercials was not considered at all appropriate.

Although the new cab, bonnet and radiator grill were being made by the Willenhall company, they were in fact of an American-influenced design and owed much to the Buick cars of the mid-1930s. The series of vertical bars on the radiator grill, which were separated by a vertical chrome strip, may have looked nice but they were not easy to clean. As most of the War Department's thinking on wartime matters then centred heavily around the threat of gas attack, it was felt that the Bedford design would be too difficult to decontaminate (clean).

As a result a more utilitarian design with angular features and flat panels was arrived at, and this became a common feature on almost all the wartime Bedford models. This design may have also had the added benefit of both saving steel and being easier to make, but it was not the reason why it was adopted as many writers on the subject have been tempted to claim. At a meeting in November 1938 the 4x4 version of the 15-cwt MW was accepted, and a further meeting was held at Luton with War Department officials in May 1939 to determine the production figures for when war was declared. In the meantime it was business as normal, and the launch of the civilian trucks was held in June 1939. The models were given considerable acclaim in the commercial motoring press of the day, but few of those esteemed journals gave any hint of the fact that the latest offerings from Bedford were really designed with a major military application in mind.

It would be virtually impossible to give an account of the Bedford models produced for the war effort, but suffice it to say that it was substantial. For this reason we are currently preparing a book *Vauxhall Went To War* for **Vauxhall Heritage Services**, which will be launched in 2002. At the end of the war hundreds (if not thousands) of MWs were released as 'war surplus', and along with the 30-cwt OXC and OXD models they were enthusiastically purchased by willing firms and individuals desperately seeking light to middle-weight commercials.

The big problem facing business was the directive to 'export or die'. This government-led export drive was seen as being an essential way to earn foreign money, which in turn was needed to pay off the crippling war debt that the country had incurred between 1939 and 1945. As a result, many of the civilian M-Type chassis that were re-introduced in 1946 were destined for overseas use, whilst hauliers and private businesses here were forced to make do with rebuilt wartime trucks. To Bedford it was big business, and as early as October 1946 the 10,000th 'export model' left Luton works for Turkey.

To get a new truck in Britain, you needed to have a good place on the Ministry of Supply's priority allocation list, or you had to face a long waiting list that ran for years rather than months or weeks. Still, many new M-Types were sold in Britain, and the model would remain in production until April 1953 when the new A-Type was launched. However, with the advent of the Big Bedford 7-ton forward control chassis at the end of 1950, the lighter variations of the M-Type were withdrawn and it was only available as a 3-tonner.

The 3-ton M-Type thus supplanted the 3-ton O-Type, as it underwent a major sea change at the start of the 1950s. First of all the OB bus was withdrawn, despite strong protests from many small operators, and the OS and OL 3-/4-ton models were uprated to 4-tons, although the OSB and OLB remained at 5-tons. As a result of the OB's demise, several operators bought the 3-ton M-Type and had it bodied for PSV use. Although it did not really have a chassis low enough for passenger work, the M-Type did a passable job, but it will long be remembered as a truly economical and dependable middle-weight commercial!

Top Left: *Here we have a 30-cwt swb M-Type in service with the Chelmsford blind, tent and marquee suppliers Godfrey. The ball tent has just been brought back to their depot by the dropside truck, and is being erected to 'dry out' after a period of hire in wet weather.*

Middle Left: *Here's one for London Transport enthusiasts, as an swb half-tilt service truck (JXC 340) pauses in a depot alongside a batch of AEC RTs. The lorry was used for general service work and repair duties, and had fleet number 895B. London Transport also had a fleet of 20-cwt M-Type service vans for the Underground railway system.*

Bottom Left: *The Brylcreem Boys would certainly have loved this M-Type 30-cwt, as it transported copious supplies of white goo in those pre-hair gel days. Calling at Maison Lesley hair salon (owned by the more ordinary sounding Mr. Long), even the driver of the van has his hair slicked back in perfect 1950 fashion!*

THE PC VAN SERIES 10- 12-CWT

The account of the PC van begins not in October 1948 when the model was 'launched', but a decade earlier with the launch of the HC in 1938 and the JC in 1939. The PC, in fact, was nothing more than a revamp of the JC and by the time it was superseded by the CA in 1952 it was certainly a very dated model.

Vauxhall's foray into small van production was nothing new, and within a few years of the move to Luton in 1905, the company were allowing body builders to put light commercial bodies on their car chassis. Those were really the first car-derived vans, but the pattern continued in the Bedford era in 1932 when the VYC and VXC models were formed on the chassis of the 17hp Vauxhall VY Cadet and the 26hp VX Cadet. These were in production from 1932 to 1935, and gave a light commercial in the 8-/12-cwt field. In 1933 the 12.8hp ASYC and the 14hp ASXC, based on the Light Six saloon gave Bedford an 8cwt van that would stay in manufacture until previously discussed new model launch of 1939.

In the latter part of 1934 the BYC and BXC model was introduced, but this was nothing more than a development of the VYC and the VXC, which were respectively given the 20hp 2,393cc and the 26.33hp 33,180cc engines of the B-series (Big Six) Vauxhall cars that had been put into production earlier that year. A smaller van, the HC (based on the Vauxhall H-Type 10/4 car) entered the scene in March 1938, although the prototype emerged in the summer of 1937. This was a lively 5- to 6-cwt model that could handle a steady 40mph at 35mpg. There was nothing really to touch it for the price, but many people found it just a bit too light for its intended purpose.

Yet the turn of speed that the HC produced made it ideally suited for newspaper delivery work, as the owners and editors of these journals aimed to get their product on to the street well ahead of their competitors. For this reason, the HC and its larger stablemate the JC were often photographed in the livery of many leading publishers of the time as many of the photographs in the Vauxhall archives clearly show. Yet the development of the H-Type car and the HC van cost Vauxhall a staggering £1 million (£54 million today).

Top Left: *Founded in 1806, the Bright & Hove Herald was a 'mild Liberal' newspaper but was also 'strongly anti-Conservative'. The journal went out of production in 1971, some two decades after their new PC van was pictured at the Pavilion in March 1950.*

Top Right: *A cracking picture for any Bedford enthusiast, this view shows the service department of Adams & Gibbon Ltd. in Newcastle. From left to right we see a 1938 WTT tipper (inside the garage), a 2¹/₂-ton O-Type breakdown wagon, a PC van (note the headboard) and an OWB bus.*

Middle Right: *The large number of body-builders and coachworks that existed in postwar Britain turned out a bewildering array of bodies on a variety of chassis. Some were wonderfully exotic, others merely functional. A good example of one of these body builders was the Huntingdon firm of Murkett Brothers, who created this Miniature Pantechnicon on a PC chassis for Peak's Furnishings of Cambridge.*

Bottom Right: *Just the thing for a book being written in the middle of a General Election, this PC 'sound car' (AHL 857) was bodied for the firm of Lodge Radiovision in Wakefield, by a local coachworks, Charles Wensley & Sons, who were based in Ings Road.*

This phenomenal investment had to be recouped, and the HC and the H cars were really designed as loss-leaders to capture the lower end of the market and break with the traditional boxy look of the earlier Bedford light vans which were, in reality, little more than modified Chevrolets. This break from the American style was followed in 1939 by an important 10-/12-cwt offering known as the JC.

This was based on the Vauxhall 12/4 I-Type car, a light-six saloon (which was in turn based on the 10hp H-Type).Clearly the investment in the 10hp model was going to be recouped in a variety of ways, and the JC van was just one example. However, it too was a model that would be stilted by the outbreak of war, but as peace returned and Vauxhall car production moved forward, the 10hp HIY car (re-introduced in 1946) went out of manufacture in 1948. This allowed the 10-/12-cwt model to move on slightly in the guise of the PC, yet in real terms little had changed. The 105-inch (2.67m) wheelbase was retained, as was much of the previous model's overall design. The front end was of all-metal construction, but the rear load-space compartment was made up from steel panelling on a hardwood frame. Whilst the design was already dated, the prices had not gone up that much either, and in 1950 a PC van cost £325 (£5,343) and a Utilecon £430 (£7,069).

In its 7-seat Utilecon version, produced by Martin Walter, the 10-/12-cwt model became very popular with the Royal Navy. The fact that the rear seats could be removed in under a minute, thus converting the 'estate car' into a van made it very popular indeed. Many were used as officer transports, and others were used by the Royal Navy hospital at Haslar. The RAF was also a large user, but by contrast the army had comparatively few. In civilian life the JC Utilecon was widely used as an ambulance, and also for police and fire-brigade applications.

Top Left: *Given that the pantechnicon shown overleaf was perhaps the ultimate extension of the 10-/12-cwt van, we now show a selection of 'loads' being put in to the basic PC van. First of all we show a load of 'Eggoroni' being carried into LNK 689 at St. Albans in 1952. Now, if you are wondering what the heck 'Eggoroni' is, I looked into the matter and found that this was basically an egg-macaroni pasta made by Avery's Vermicelli Ltd.*

Middle Left: *Now this is a load that might be more easily recognised, as a line up of four PC vans stand outside the London Blood Supply Centre of the National Blood Transfusion Service at Sutton. The insulated boxes carried baskets of dried blood, which will be distributed to hospitals throughout London during the day ahead.*

Bottom Left: *A load of old bollards - no not the text in this caption - rather the load in the back of this PC (KLA 620), which is working for the Royal Borough of Kensington on 1st October 1950.*

The 'new' PC van employed the four-cylinder 1,442cc engine of the Wyvern LIX model, but it is understood that a very small number were experimentally fitted with the larger 2275cc six-cylinder engine from the Velox LIP. The PC had the three-speed gearboxes that were fitted to both of the L model cars, and also employed their steering-column gear change lever instead of the floor-mounted lever of the JC. Whilst this may have been fashionable and essential on a saloon car with a bench seat, it was neither practical nor well-liked in the van variant. Another fashion change, reflecting the desire for better electrical performance, was the change from a 6-volt to a 12-volt electrical system.

In terms of fuel economy the PC scored exceptionally well, and a road test in the *Commercial Motor* magazine stated that the van returned an average of 39mpg when hauling an 11-cwt load at just under 30mph. The load space of 110 cubic feet was acceptable for most small business uses, but some enterprising body builders saw a chance to expand this capacity by adding Luton bodies to the chassis.

The speed and capacity of the PC once again made it an attractive proposition for newspaper proprietors, and it seems that Bedford dealers were instructed to give better discounts to publishers who purchased the model (if only that were the case today)! The thinking behind this idea was obviously associated with the publicity that these vans would attract, as they were literally moving adverts travelling around the city streets. In those days most newspaper vans would carry billboards showing the latest news headlines - such as 'Man Bites Dog' or 'Chancellor Increases Purchase Tax' - which immediately grabbed the public attention in those pre-electronic message days.

In fact people often looked out for a newspaper van to keep abreast of latest developments, especially if they were too hard-pressed to actually buy a newspaper or go down to the local Odeon or Gaumont to watch Pathe News on the cinema screen. Vauxhall therefore concluded that newspaper vans were a good medium to catch the public eye, and the policy of discounted prices on such vehicles continued with the CA models well into the 1950s!

But it was not just in newspaper work that the PC excelled, but in almost every form of commercial activity. From small one-man corner shops to larger organisations such as the Co-operative Wholesale Society, the PC was well liked by the retail trade. In fact with the CWS being such a fond user of the PC van, many of the local Co-operative retail societies followed suit. As such the PC became everything from a delivery van to a mobile shop, as one of the pictures show.

The model was well-liked by several brewery firms, others were converted into milk floats, and a few became ice-cream vans, but so far pictures of this application have been hard to find - unlike the CA which literally became the ice cream man's favourite chassis. I even recall one running as a mobile bookshop in the rural part of the West Riding of Yorkshire when I was a boy, operated by the book-sellers Reid & Co., who I think also had a couple of HC mobile libraries as well. Sometime in the mid-1950s the Reid van stopped calling at Meltham Mills Primary School, and it was replaced by a grey and cream mobile library operated by West Riding County Council. At this point it is perhaps appropriate to give a plug to the books on mobile libraries and ice cream vans that also appear in the **Nostalgia Road** series.

The PC was never widely employed by the Post Office (either telephones or the Royal Mail), but examples did appear in both fleets. Yet, by contrast, they were widely used by both public utility companies (gas, water and electric) and by many local authorities. Again an odd contrast is found in the fact that I have not discovered any PCs in the British Railways fleet, but at the same time there were a large number at work with British Road Services. True, a number of these were inherited with fleets acquired by the nationalisation of road haulage, but at the same time it is clear that many new ones were purchased between 1948 and the discontinuation of the PC model in 1952. The fact that the PC was really the only light-weight post-war commercial offering from Bedford had placed a lot on its shoulders, it was a relatively light construction and the steel was not of the best quality, especially in the 1950-2 built models, so comparatively few have survived into preservation - but if you know of one lurking in a barn somewhere!!!!!

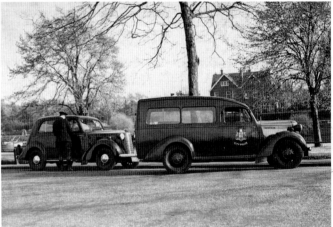

Top Right: *Now it may well become obvious, as you pass through this book, that I like pictures of vehicles at work, and the more unusual the setting the better. This superb period picture taken in the Scottish coalfield is a really evocative image that shows a service long since forgotten. Here the Mussleburgh & Fisherrow Co-operative Society uses SY 9827, one of its five PC vans, as a mobile Butchery Shop.*

Middle Right: *The 'estate' version of the PC produced by Martin Walter was known as the Utilecon, and it came with two side window options, both of which are shown on this page. First of all we have the long window example, as seen in this Radio Car in service with Nottingham City Police in 1949.*

Bottom Right: *Widely used in emergency service work, the Utilecon also made a good ambulance, as seen at Northallerton Ambulance Station in the North Riding of Yorkshire on 30th January 1953.*

THE CA SERIES 10- 12-CWT (1952-1959)

If you purchased this book expecting it to be full of words and pictures on the Bedford CA, then I have to say that we are sorry to disappoint you. Although the CA was undoubtedly *the* light commercial of the 1950s and 1960s, it can only form a very small part of this account. Indeed some may feel aggrieved that such an important subject has only warranted nine pages, as this particular semi-forward control model really deserves a book in its own right.

The authors would wholeheartedly agree with that sentiment, and such a volume will hopefully be produced in the **Nostalgia Road-Classic Marques** series in the not too distant future. For the present though, the nine pages that follow are really only a brief introduction to the subject at hand. In some ways the CA was a logical successor to the PC model, but its wider applications as light commercial undoubtedly derives from those users who had begun their businesses with those rebuilt ex-WD MWs in the second half of the 1940s. In fact it was this market that Vauxhall had clearly identified when it came up with the idea of offering the CA not just as a factory built van, but as a chassis cab or chassis cowl also!

Top Left: *As may be imagined, Vauxhall Motors took hundreds of pictures of the CA between 1952 and 1969, and this presented a great difficulty when it came to making a selection for the images to be used in this book. The pictures that follow are therefore a representative collection and not a comprehensive one. I hope that a* **Nostalgia Road** *book will appear on this model in the not too distant future, when I can have 'free-reign' on the picture content. Meanwhile, here is a really good Bedford picture, showing a MkI CA belonging to Scats agricultural merchants. A line up of at least nine newer CA vans stands to the right, along with two brand new TK trucks. In the background are two more of the firm's lorries, with a Fordson diesel and a Bedford S-Type diesel.*

Bottom Left: *The basis for many special bodies, the CA chassis/cowl was built in quite large numbers and seen here in detail. Many of these chassis/cowls became ice cream vans or mobile shops, and in our companion book* Fifty Years Of Ice Cream Vans, *we have a picture of two such chassis shortly after their arrival at the Cummins factory in Crewe.*

Top Right: *The CA was seen as a 'Jack of all trades', and it certainly sold well into both the construction industry and the municipal authority markets, where light trucks were in big demand. This Walker pick-up truck conversion was just one of the applications for the CA which endeared it to builders everywhere. It will be noted from the trio of pictures on this page, that not all CA models had the sliding door arrangement of the 10-/12-cwt van. Obviously as the van side was an integral part of the support for the sliding door arrangement, the chassis cab versions all had traditional slam doors. Similarly, many Luton vans, ice cream vans, mobile shops and so on, all had the conventional doors, which were supplied by Vauxhall as an 'extra' that could be purchased with the chassis-cowl.*

Middle Right: *One step up from the pick-up, and what no self-respecting builder or Parks & Gardens supervisor could do without, was this handy little tipper truck based on the CA. Again bodied by Walkers, this chunky little beast is seen in a photograph dated November 1952.*

Bottom Right: *The final variant of load capability was the flat-bed, which in various forms, suited a variety of applications. Now the problem with the flat bed was the fact that the top of the rear wheel arches would have stood much higher than the bed of the platform if it was mounted directly to the chassis. If a low height deck was required, this meant that two box-like protrusions would have to stand above the platform. For applications like milk floats and so on, this was not really a major problem, but for heavier loads like coal or agricultural goods a flat deck was essential. This is well illustrated in this picture of a CA platform truck employed by the Barnstaple coal merchants Andrew & Knell. Note the intermediary timber frame supporting the flat-bed platform.*

Top Left: *Having discussed doors in the previous set of photograph captions, I should have mentioned that the slam (or hinged) door arrangement came in two varieties, normal front hinged doors or rear hinged (suicide) doors. The optional door packs had mountings for either end, but some builders like Smiths Delivery Vehicles of Gateshead only ordered the driver's side door. On mobile shops and ice cream vans in particular, no off-side door was fitted as a front passenger seat was not needed. This allowed access to the rear sales area in the van, and also the fitting of a small wash-hand basin in the cab. The lack of an off-side cab is well illustrated in this picture of a Smith's 'Viandette' mobile butcher's shop.*

Middle Left: *The suicide door, so called because rear-hinged doors could blow open whilst travelling, is well illustrated in this Luton-bodied van built by Grosvenor. For service with Peck of Ampthill, the van is seen just before delivery to the furnishing company. But, just look at that telephone number, a single digit, doesn't that say something about how times have changed since January 1954.*

Bottom Left: *Some of the conversions to the CA retained much of the basic body shell, and this is well illustrated by this picture of the Grosvenor CA Canopy Pick-up. This model was basically a cut down van, that was supplied without rear doors. The cutting points are quite obvious from this picture, but only the top of the new drop-down tailgate can be observed. This pick-up was well liked by builders, but it looked even better as a breakdown truck/service van, a role for which many carried a small crane or winch.*

I suppose my first recollection of the CA would be a 1957 model Dormobile, with a porthole window that my father had on loan from the Red Sign Garage at Moseley in 1961 whilst his new Ford Anglia was sent back to Dagenham for 'works attention'. The CA had lost its internal camper van fittings, but oddly it still had the sink and had gained a row of cinema seats (complete with the tilting cushions) transversely bolted (rather insecurely) to the van's floor along one side. Thus, with our eight-seat bus, we set off along the A635 bound for home. However, half way across the Pennines and in the middle of the notorious Saddleworth Moor the beast broke down. No sooner than it did so, a thick moorland mist came rolling across the bogs and we set off walking for the Isle of Skye. No, that isn't the famous island off the West Coast of Scotland, but the name of a moorland pub above Holmfirth which had been demolished in the 1950s. Still, its site had a emergency roadside 'phone box (either AA or RAC, I forget which) and we went to summon help. No cars passed us in the two-mile trek, and we were chilled to the bone despite its being mid-August. When we got to the 'box, my dad looked for his RAC key to open the door, only to realise that it, along with his Anglia, was already heading south to Essex. Never had I heard my father use such bad language, and a further two-mile trek ensued as we headed down to Meltham. Fish and chips in Wessendenhead Road soothed the inner man, but never did I hear my father speak kindly about Bedford vans after that!

Yet the the MkI CA was really the van of the 1950s, and it broke new ground in its field! It had burst on to the market as a 10-/12- cwt van, but it also came in either chassis cowl or chassis cab versions to suit specialist body-building applications. Other body builders adapted the standard van to create an amazing variety of vehicles from the one basic van, including a London Taxi in a conversion (by Grosvenor)! A few of the more common conversions are shown in the accompanying pictures.

It was originally powered with a 1507cc 'square' four-cylinder petrol engine, as employed in the Vauxhall E-Type Wyvern saloons (1951-1957) then in production. The basic van enjoyed 135-cubic feet of load space, and its wide, sliding front doors gave easy access to the cab. Ease of access was continued by the 16-inch road wheels, which gave a low loading height, but this was improved even further in 1957 when 15-inch wheels became the standard fitment. The same 1957 revamp saw the aging 1507cc engine being ousted in place of the 1507cc engine that Vauxhall was fitting in the new F-Type Victor saloon cars.

The initial price was £400 plus Purchase Tax, making a grand total of £481, which would work out at about a little under £8,000 in today's money. The one big drawback that the van had, was its original split screen form, and some body builders began offering a one-piece screen on chassis-cowl conversions from the mid-1950s onward. The main market where this seemed to take place was in the field of ice cream vans and mobile shops, where large expanses of glass were almost obligatory. Obviously, much more could be said about the MkI CA, but as this forms the basis of a forthcoming book in this series, we trust that you will bear with this brief introduction given to it herein.

Top Right: *One development of the CA van was its conversion into a crew-bus, mini-bus, ambulance or caravanette. Conversions were first achieved by removing the indented rear side panel in the upper half of the van's body shell. This feature was part of the initial design for the body shell, and came about following extensive discussions with Martin Walter who, up to 1952, had been converting the PC into the Utilecon. Here we see the Martin Walter conversion of the CA, which makes use of the whole area contained in the recessed panel.*

Middle Right: *By contrast with the Martin Walter offering, the estate car version of the CA that was produced by Grosvenor used two smaller window panes. This had the effect of making the rear window 'fall short' of the recessed panel and created quite a poor effect. In reality the Grosvenor (and some of the Kenex models) looked like conversions, whereas the Martin Walter did not!*

Bottom Right: *I really should have included that other Martin Walter product in this section, namely the Dormobile caravanette, but this subject is to be covered in a **Nostalgia Road** book on camper vans during 2002. I therefore opted for this picture of a 'Lancastrian II Minor Ambulance' produced by Levers for Buckinghamshire County Council in 1954. This subject is also covered in a Trans-Pennine book (NHS Ambulances 1948-1973), as the CA became a very popular choice with ambulance services all over the country.*

THE CA SERIES 15-CWT (1959-1969)

There is no doubt that the Ford Transit became one of the most popular light commercials of all time, and from the late 1960s to the present day it has really dominated the British van scene. Yet had you asked anyone at the start of the 1960s what was the most popular light commercial then, the answer would have been the Bedford CA. Inside just seven years it had revolutionised the market place, and all the giant motor manufacturers, Ford, Austin-Morris, Commer and Standard were trying to emulate the success that Vauxhall had enjoyed since 1952.

Yet by the end of the 1950s, the Bedford CA was already getting long in the tooth, and a major facelift was needed to take the model into the 'Swinging Sixties'. The improvements that came about in the later CAs should chronologically go elsewhere in this book, but as they are so closely associated with the 1952-models, it is logical to consider these at this point in our narrative.

The mechanical changes, based on technology developed for the new range of Vauxhall cars in 1957 was at the heart of the changes intended for the van. Yet the biggest complaint from customers was the cosmetic issue of the two-piece windscreen. As a consequence, Vauxhall obtained a one-piece glass screen that Smiths Delivery Vehicles were fitting to ice cream vans and mobile shops at its Gateshead factory in 1957. This was essentially a flat piece of glass, but it was fitted to a test van and sent on a series of trial runs before being sent out to three dealers in the North London area for evaluation. A very favourable response was generated, and as it eliminated a potential blind spot, Vauxhall's windscreen suppliers were asked to make a new one-piece screen for the CA. However, as opposed to its being flat, the Bedford design envisaged a panoramic curved window, with the manufacturers using the same technology as they were doing in the new F-Type Victors and PA Crestas. I am not sure when the first of these was fitted to a CA for testing, but it could have been in the autumn of 1957.

Top Left: *The development of the CA became essential as the 1950s progressed, and by the end of the decade a new range of models were put on show. In this pre-release photograph taken in November 1959, we see from left to right on the front row the Osborne milk float £573.00 (£6,847), the Walker Vanorama drop side truck £540.00 (£6,453), the Kenebrake 12-seater minibus £633.00 (£7,564) and on the back row a basic 15-cwt van £480.00 (£5,736), the Martin Walter Utilabus £573.00 (£6,847), a diesel 15-cwt van £605.00 (£7,229) and a Grosvenor Canopy Pick-up at £569.00 (£6,799).*

Top Right: *Complete with roof advertising boards proclaiming a special offer of one shilling per pound off GP Tea, a standard 15-cwt van calls at the grocery shop of C.J.Fordham, 38 Harper Road. In addition to the advertising for Paynes Tea & Coffee that is carried on WLD 211, the grocery shop window is a veritable treasure-house of 1959 advertising. Amongst the displays are posters for Bovril, Cadbury's Half Covered Biscuits, Ambrosia Creamed Rice, Jaffa Juice, and Bovril Corned Beef.*

Middle Right: *Working at a Midlands Electricity Board depot, this CA dropside truck (2219 HA), was typical of the hundreds of Bedford light commercials employed by the nationalised utility companies in Britain at that time. Several pictures of these types of vehicles will appear in our books in the* **Nostalgia Road - Famous Fleets** *series dealing with the gas industry and the electricity supply services. One picture that has been saved for the electric book is a fascinating view of a CA being used as an articulated tractor towing a delivery van body for the Yorkshire Electricity Board - I kid you not.*

Bottom Right: *My recollections of the CA are not all that favourable, for in my days as a hard-up and penniless student, I had a part-time job with a close family friend Ronnie, who used a CA dropside like this as one of his coal delivery vehicles. So, when I talked about the high loading height of the bed above the wheels, I know from painful experience what I am talking about. It was superb for getting sacks of coal on to your shoulders, but it was a real chore lifting them up from the ground where they had been bagged at the start of the day.*

With the screen improvements resolved and the engine and gearbox up-rated, the humble 10-/12-cwt specification was under-selling what the van could really achieve. Therefore, from 1959 onwards a MkII version appeared. It now featured the one-piece screen and a revised radiator grill to complement the mechanical changes, but at the same time there was a stretched version of the CA being put through secret testing. Originally the CA had a 90-inch (2.28m) wheelbase, but many owners and a large number of body-builders claimed that this was too short for what their customers were specifying, (oddly enough the most vociferous were those building milk floats or gown/Luton vans). As a result Bedford launched a 102-inch (2.59m) long wheelbase version providing 171 cubic feet of load space. This was designated the CAL, whilst the old model became known as the CAS.

Top Left: *Moving now to special bodies on the MkII CA, we begin with this picture of a chassis-cowl photographed at the works for publicity purposes. This picture illustrates the changes from the earlier MkI chassis-cowl, but the most obvious difference is the single-piece windscreen, obviously a big improvement over the original design. Note the wooden box delivery driver's seat.*

Middle Left: *Imagine, driving that chassis cowl all the way from Luton to Reading in the dead of winter, no protection from the elements, a basic seat, and nothing to stop you falling out. Well that is what happened to some poor soul who had the job of taking this chassis to Vincent's coach builders. The finished 'high-top' van went into service with the Midlands Electricity Board as 2228 HA, and was used for delivering electrical appliances from showrooms to their customers.*

Bottom Left: *Mind you, not every CA chassis left Bedfordshire under their own power, quite the contrary for they were also taken by road transporter and also by rail. The rail service often saw vans and chassis being moved on flat wagons, but these were usually in mixed trains that would include saloon cars and heavier trucks as well. This picture is therefore quite remarkable, as it shows no less than 100 CAs leaving Luton for Martin Walter's at Folkestone. Some were destined to become mini-buses, others would be turned into campers, but this view well illustrates the phenomenal number of Bedfords that could be sent to this one company alone at that time. Sadly steam obscures the number on the British Railways Standard Class 9F 2-10-0 locomotive hauling the train.*

The one-fifth increase in load capacity of the CAL over the CAS may have proved very useful to most owners, but as usual there were always those who were wanting to take their vehicles beyond their physical capabilities, and this was perhaps nowhere more true than in the construction industry where the CA had become the main workhorse. As the late-1950s and 1960s were a boom-time for British builders, the number of CAs working in this sector was staggering. Yet dealers were repeatedly reporting that many of the engine and gearbox problems being dealt with under warranty, were actually a consequence of undue load being placed on the existing power unit and transmission.

As a result of this Bedford design engineers looked at what could be done. One of those involved (Ron) said:- 'As the engine changes had come into place to up rate the old square-fours, we knew that it would not be long before owners were asking too much of the new unit. There were a lot of problems with the chain-driven crankshaft, and a lot of side wear in the pistons as well. When you looked at an engine that had come back for examination, you could tell that they had been getting really hot. Hammered might be an appropriate description. What we really needed was a nice little diesel engine in the front, but Vauxhall had no in-house contender. At that time we were using Leyland for power units on the bigger commercials then being planned, as for example the 400cu unit on the new VAL bus chassis.'

In the early part of 1960 we were experimenting with three diesel engines, including one from the USA, but the really obvious contender was the 4-99 unit from Perkins. This was given a really severe testing both on the test track and also in the field, but it took all the knocks it was given and then came back for more.' It is not surprising to report that this was the unit that was fitted in to the CA from the middle of 1961 onwards. Even so it was not a cheap option as it cost £605.00 (£7,229) a good £125 (£1,493) more than its petrol engined counterpart. Even so other changes were also in the offing, most notable was the provision of a four-speed, all synchromesh gearbox, and as such it became the first British-made light van to enjoy this facility.

Improvements to the model came again both in 1963 and 1964, but these were more updates than anything really radical, though the fitting of radios became a popular optional extra. Yet, I suppose the one thing that made this what the press again described as 'The Roundsman's Van', were those 39-inch wide sliding doors on the CAL. I remember both their ease of access and the thrill you got driving around in the height of summer with both doors open. The rush of air, the freedom of the open road, and not a seat belt in sight; were we mad or just insane?

The facelift given to the final version of the CA remains (in my opinion) unsurpassed in the field of light commercial vehicles in Britain. The CAs design gave the impression of its being the scaled down version of a big truck or van, and to this writer at least, that is what a light commercial should look like. Smooth flowing curves, a decent amount of chromium finish, and a cab that was a delight to sit in. Alright, by the end of their production life they weren't in the least modern, but they were *the* van of the early 1960s. As with the earlier model CA, there is much to be said and nowhere near enough space to say it. Yet one accolade that must be given to the CA, is the fond place it still has in many people's minds, for in addition to being a businessman's or worker's vehicle, it was also a child's van as well.

Top Right: *Another builder on the CA chassis was Smith's Delivery Vehicles, and we have already seen their Viandette travelling shop. For ice cream men, they had their Cornette range, and here we show one of these on a MkII chassis. This was one of just 36 CAs operated by E. Cappoci of Airdrie, and it would travel on regular rounds in a 30-mile radius of the town. The Smith's van had the capacity for a good revenue earning run, as it was capable of carrying 50-gallons of ice cream, lollies, soft drinks, crisps and sweets.*

Middle Right: *This 1959 view shows a close up picture of the Osborne Dairy Vehicle, lettered in the livery of the Fernhurst Dairy. The milk float carries slogans to be displayed at the Earls Court Commercial Motor Show, which proclaim 'Bedford The Practical Van', 'Easy Entry & Exit', 'Full-View Windscreen', 'Easy Parking' and 'Economy of Operation'.*

Bottom Right: *The Martin Walter 'Utilabus' conversion, is featured in this rather nice 1961 picture in service with the Norton Works Motorcycle Racing team.*

Whilst my childhood memories of that 1957 loan CA may not have been that fond, two complete generations of kids grew up knowing the CA as a 'fun' vehicle. In its Dormobile guise it took them on holiday, in its mini-bus guise it took them on day trips, but it was as an ice cream van that it really scored with a young audience.

Having co-written the first ever history of ice cream mobiles, in conjunction with Stuart Whitby (the owner of the largest ice cream van body-builders in Europe today), this is a subject that I have come to know quite intimately. From this viewpoint I can state quite categorically that for a very large number of people in this trade, there will never, ever be another light commercial like the Bedford CA.

This view is also held by fellow Bedford enthusiasts, and some superb examples are still in daily work in kinder climates where rust has not eaten away at the stylish body work, Fortunately a good number of CAs are now preserved, despite the economy of their original build (that's a kind way of saying that the CAs often rusted badly), but those that had fibreglass or coachbuilt bodies fared much better - in fact I know where there is a lovely CA with a glass-fibre high-top Martin Walter mini-bus body just begging to be restored and salvaged from its present role as a peat store in the Shetlands. The same is true with many models supplied to warmer climes or places where road salt was not extensively used, and many of these would make very easy restoration programmes for those who can afford the shipping costs!

In practical terms the CA was replaced by the CF in 1969, but in many people's affections it will ever reign supreme.

Top Left: *In the final major change to the CA range, a number of refinements were added to effectively create a MkIII version. This would stay in production until 1969, when it was replaced by the Bedford CF and so a succession of new models (CB, CD, and CE) never came to fruition. Sadly (to my personal view) the CF never had the flair of the CA nor the gutsy performance of its all-conquering rival the Ford Transit, which had appeared on the scene in 1965.*

Middle Left: *The facelift given to the final version of the CA remains unsurpassed in the field of light commercial vehicles in Britain. Here the attractive design of the CA is coupled with an odd contraption owned by Trans World Airlines. It is, of course, a set of mobile steps used at airports around the world. The upper part of the stairs retracts into the lower half, and a large 'sun-roof' allows the driver to have perfect visibility of this operation. The skirt running round the truck carries the four stabilising jacks, one of which is mounted at each corner.*

Bottom Left: *Finally, this CA chassis carries one of the ugliest looking bodies ever put on the model. Alright opinion is subjective, but this Walker Fineline glass-fibre bread van cannot have many fans. Aesthetics aside, this combination did have a significant carrying capacity, and this particular van had an unladen weight of 1-ton, 11-cwt and 3-lbs. It was operated by Tony Morgan of Timplings Row, Hemel Hempstead.*

Above: *Here we have a second series CA van, photographed in September 1959 in readiness for a new brochure that was to be released that November to promote the 10/12-cwt and 15-cwt Bedford vans. This is a CAL, long wheelbase model, has a 102 inch wheel base and 171 cubic feet of load space. Bedford's proved and tested features had put them at the front of light van technology at this time. By the date this brochure was produced, the company were able to boast that they had already built 140,000 light vans, and their reliability was widely recognised.*

Right: *Although the CA may not be as comfortable as today's offerings, its easy access and egress can still teach modern van designers a great deal. As this picture clearly shows, the wonderfully wide doorways could accommodate even the largest of drivers, not to mention ease of loading through the front doors as well as those at the rear.*

Above: *By the end of the period under consideration, Bedford had moved on to its third CA, and it would not be long before the CF was introduced. The HA Viva van had also appeared, but this time sporting conventional hinged doors. However the sliding doors were welcomed by drivers who had to do delivery/collection work in confined spaces, and when placing an order for 'evaluation' models of the HA, both British Railways and the GPO enquired whether or not a sliding door version could be produced. This view shows an interesting comparison between the CA and HA.*

Right: *Illustrating the colourful livery that some owners adopted at the time, a striking black and yellow scheme is seen on this 1966 CA owned by the builders R. B. Tyler (Ware) Ltd. The door windows on this model had some 60% more glass than found on the original CA and the Series II CAS. Thus giving far better visibility for the driver!*

Above: *Recorded as a prototype HA van, this picture shows the car-derived van produced by Bedford around their popular HA Viva. It shared many components with the saloon car, but a number of items were different including the front doors. This boxy little commercial quickly became a firm favourite with all manner of firms, not least of which were big organisations like British Rail, British Gas, regional electric companies, and GPO Telephones (British Telecom), although the HA never made big inroads into the BMC-dominated fleet of the GPO's Royal Mail operation.*

Right: *Although outside the time frame of this particular book, we use this view of a 1968 HA van to illustrate a typical 'fleet owner'. Here we see MRV 531G of Bass Charrington Brewers which was allocated to their Lockwood Depot near Huddersfield. We are not sure where this picture is actually taken, but with National Petrol a 6s 7d per gallon who cares. This one is for you Chris!*

Above: *The variety of bodies applied to the CA chassis is well illustrated in this book, and we can see this included everything from mini-buses to ambulances and from milk floats to ice cream vans (all subjects of* **Nostalgia Road** *books). However it may not be readily appreciated, but the HA was also offered in a number of modified forms. None of these came as factory-built units, but body-builders all around the country did some wonderful conversions, quite often with the approval of Bedford. Milk floats, hot-dog vans, ice cream vans, pick-up trucks, Dormobile camper vans (the Roma), plate-glass carriers, and gown vans like this one pictured here. The possibilities were beyond permutation, so no wonder that the HA became such a popular little van!*

28

THE TA-TYPE 20-CWT TO 30-CWT

The year 1950 marked a big turning point in Bedford's fortunes, for after this it entered into the serious commercial vehicle world when the firm launched its S-Type 7-ton chassis at the Commercial Motor Show. Now they had a really modern forward control chassis, which utilised the new six-cylinder 84bhp petrol engine that they had introduced in the spring. The O-Type, a real Bedford stalwart, was threatened by this arrival and the first casualty was the OB bus chassis. The lorry chassis would last a while longer, but Bedford had clearly seen that a new range of light- to middle-weight commercials were needed for the 1950s. A major improvement was given to the O-, K- and M- types, when a new gearbox was introduced with synchromesh between second, third and fourth gears. These models are identified by the large radiator badge and a black vertical dividing strip replacing the chrome one on earlier radiators.

Above: *This line-up of Bedford vehicles is fairly typical of the situation in many large fleets in the mid-1950s. It shows the Commercial Street Depot of the East Midlands Gas Board on 16th November 1955 after a pair of brand new 30-cwt A-Types had been delivered. At that date the board's fleet boasted 32 Bedfords, including the WS and PC models seen here. The two new A-Type tankers were used for cleaning out gas mains in Sheffield.*

Those three models had given sterling service, and by 1953 nearly half a million had been built, but it was a design from the 1930s! It was thus no surprise when their successors appeared in the new TA-Type range in the spring of 1953 (invariably this series was better known as simply the A-Type). Inheriting many of the mechanical features from the latter O-, K- and M- types, the A-Type was aimed at the 1-ton to 4-ton range. The models of 3-ton and below inherited the 76bhp engine, and the bigger ones got the 84bhp version.

Top Left: *In a caption that read 'Wherever there is a ship to repair, this new 2-tonner run by the New Medway Steam Packet Company can be sent with machinery and fitters'. This particular view was taken at Farrell's Creek, with one of their ships,* Queen of the Channel *behind. The A-Type seen here was actually a 35-cwt model.*

Middle Left: *A conventional A-Type 25-cwt van (PYH 473) hauls a twin-axle trailer as part of the Advance Publicity unit of Bertram Mills Circus. Its duties, as will be obvious from the lettering on the van, was the road sign service that the company provided before the circus came to town. I am not sure whether this van and trailer would have been painted in a two-tone green colour scheme or a green and grey one, as it changed from one to the other around this time.*

Bottom Left: *In addition to having a van with just a rear-loading door, it was becoming obvious that side loading doors were a big advantage. These three-way loading vans were nothing new, and we have already seen a three-way door M-Type in this book carrying Brylcreem. Yet, in conjunction with the body builders Spurling, Bedford found that the three-way loading van was a good selling feature. This one was used by Moors Market of Southport for the collection of soft fruits from local market gardens during the summer season. Larger consignments of vegetables (especially potatoes) would have been handled by the firm's O-Type and S-Type lorries.*

What was a major difference was the all new integral steel cab, which was clearly designed to complement the cab designed for both the S-Type range and the new CA vans. Although the normal control arrangement necessitated the retention of a bonnet, the A-Type broke with the convention of the long, narrow nosed designs used since 1931. In many ways it had a distinctly American look about it, and it had GM (Chevrolet) origins. The British cab featured a two-piece windscreen, whilst the bonnet had broad wings with integral headlamps and in early models it had its sidelights incorporated within a decorative wing flash.

Whilst only the models under the 3-ton capacity concern us here, we should mention that there were four basic chassis ranging from 119-inches (3m) to 167-inches (4.25m). There was also an 8-ton tractor unit, but this shared the same chassis as the swb 4-ton truck. In carrying capacity, the A-Type was designed to nominally meet the following payload requirements 1-ton to 1¼-ton, 1½-ton to 2-ton, 3-ton, 4-ton and 5-ton. Of course there was the 8-ton tractor unit, but anything over a rigid 5-ton would be catered for by the S-Type. It was a complex arrangement, but it did utilise a lot of common components across a wide range of vehicles, and in turn resulted in considerable economies in both build and design costs. This philosophy had obviously been proved correct in the new range of models introduced just before World War II, and it was to continue through the A- and D- types right down to the TJ series. It seems a little complicated at first, and it wasn't always easy to tell which models were which. Two easy clues are the single wheels on the rear axles of the smaller A-Types and the factory-fitted diesel engines (as an option) to the 4- and 5-ton models.

As a successor to the K- and M- types, the lightweight A-Type models often found themselves working on the same duties as their predecessors. In fact, so reliable and economical had the earlier models been, that when it came time to replace them, operators naturally chose the corresponding A-Type model. The picture at the East Midlands Gas Board depot shown earlier is a good example, for it clearly illustrates model continuity in the fleet of one obviously satisfied Bedford owner.

In 1954, the sale of Bedfords had reached yet another peak, with an aggregate of 1,121 models being turned out every week, or put another way, an average of 160 commercials a day, seven days a week. Luton was simply bursting at the seams, but an answer had already been identified out at Dunstable, where Vauxhall had their Parts & Accessories Division. A new plant was built at Dunstable, with commercial vehicle production thereafter being concentrated on this site. It opened in the summer of 1955, and on the second day of August, the first truck rolled off the new assembly line.

Fittingly, the first truck off the line was the A-Type pictured on this page. With the opening of Dunstable, the 2-/3-ton models became light commercials, after they were re-classed as 2-tonners. A new 3-ton lwb chassis was introduced, but it too was classed as a lightweight. The 4-ton to 6-ton models became middle-weights, and the 7-tonners were heavy-weights. But it gets even more confusing, as (in 1956) the lighter end of the range saw their designations changed to 25-cwt and 35-cwt. Other changes were announced as well, including the arrival of a diesel engine for all the A-Type models. On the smaller lightweights this unit was the 55bhp Perkins P4 unit.

Top Right: *This June 1954 view of a 20-cwt A-Type chassis cab shows it in service as an aviation fuel bowser with Shell-Mex & British Petroleum. With its short wheelbase and long bonneted cab, the vehicle looks well out of proportion, but aviation spirit was (is) quite heavy and with the associated pumping equipment, the vehicle (when loaded) was probably at the maximum range of its capacity.*

Middle Right: *As my home town is Huddersfield, I was delighted to find this view of a mobile shop supplied to Henderson's Grocers of Kirkburton. I can remember this van running around the rural villages south of Huddersfield, but did not know it had a body by Westmorland of Wakefield until I found this fine picture in the archives at Luton. The chassis was a 20-cwt model modified to forward control by Neville's of Mansfield and finished up with an unladen weight of 2-ton, 7-cwt 3-lbs. Note the superimposed bumper on this picture!*

Bottom Right: *The final view of an A-Type should be a milestone picture, and this view taken on 2nd August 1955 certainly is. For this was the first truck to come off the new bus and truck assembly line that Vauxhall had built at Dunstable. The firm had been based in the town for some time, but only for parts and not manufacture. Therefore chassis number 729,539 was exceptionally significant for both Dunstable and Luton as it freed up much needed space at the Vauxhall plan for car production.*

THE TD-TYPE 25-CWT TO 2-TON

Really, if we were to follow Bedford's classification, the heading for this chapter should include 3-ton, as the firm now viewed it as a light commercial. Just 20 years earlier this had been the firm's heaviest commercial, and this one fact shows how things had really changed in just two decades. The 1956 weight category changes had really been a preamble for what was to follow next, the new Bedford TD-Type (again better known as the D-Type). I say new with some reservation, because so much of the A-Type was carried forward, that visually the two were almost identical. It is probably more correct to say is that this was a re-designation, that came about because Bedford were now to offer a forward control version of the A-Type.

Firms like G.E. Neville of Mansfield had been converting Bedford trucks to forward control since World War II and possibly before (although I will stand corrected on that point). Neville often worked closely with a firm called Baico Patents Ltd., who fitted chassis extensions to the forward control chassis conversions. This service was well used by coach- and body-builders making fire engines, mobile libraries, dustcarts and mobile shops (as for example that shown on the Westmorland bodied A-Type shown earlier). It wasn't a lucrative market, but it was a steady one.

Bedford obviously had their eyes on a factory-built forward control middle-weight, and probably for good reason. The reason was not so much to do with the commercial field, but the bus market, where they had alienated a lot of loyal Bedford operators when they killed off the OB bus chassis in 1950. Whilst most progressive firms wanted a 33-seat coach, many more were quite content with a 27- to 29-seat vehicle, and the demise of the OB really created a few problems, especially in rural areas. Bedford tried to get round this by offering a conversion of the OL lorry chassis, but with the arrival of the A-Type the bus buyers were really fuming.

A few buses were built on the A-Type chassis, as we show in our companion book *Bedford Buses of the 1950s & '60s*, but these were ungainly, ugly and thus not very well liked in general. The bus chassis team repeatedly brought this fact to management's attention, as did Bedford's close working partners, Duple Motors of Hendon.

Duple had long profited from the OB-Duple Vista combination, and they wanted it back. The answer was to make a forward control version of the A-Type, and the ideal chassis to modify was the ubiquitous 4-tonner. A prototype was built and fitted with a scaled down version of Duple's Vega body with its distinctive side-flash and 'butterfly grill'. It was an instant success, and it was soon planned to be launched as the 'New Vista' 29-seater.

Top Left: *The successor to the A-Type was the D-Type, and it was visually little different from the model introduced in 1952. Subtle differences in indicators and sidelights were an obvious clue, as many of the A-Type models used the same oblong frosted glass sidelights (mounted in chrome brackets) that featured on the S-Type lorries and the SB bus. Indicators appeared above the bumper bar, whilst (from 1955) the sidelights were mounted on stalks atop the wing. However, as external bodybuilding of Bedford's carried on in a major way, even these changes were not automatic. Some of the features mentioned above can be seen in this May 1958 view at Renfrew Airport. Here a 2-ton van in service with British European Airways overtakes a stationary PA Cresta parked by the 'No Waiting' sign.*

Top Right: *The prototype D-Type 35-cwt/2-ton chassis-cowl with a short wheelbase chassis and twin rear wheels.*

Middle Right: *The rear end view of the Walker pick-up conversion on the D-Type chassis, giving a model that has a real American look about it - was this a result of GMs parentage? Functional in a number of applications, the big drawback on this model were the rear lights which, being unprotected, tended to get smashed off quite easily.*

Bottom Right: *The same model of 25-cwt pick-up truck, albeit in a different colour and fitted with the Perkins diesel engine (although not badged as such). It also has several optional extras, including the chrome bumper bar and wheel hubs. This photograph was taken at the end of 1956, but it carries the legend 'Not To Be Published Before 14th February 1957'.*

I have a copy of the first advertising mock-up, and it is full of superlatives, but yet it does not mention that the new C-Type chassis would also feature 5- and 6-ton models. Perhaps this had not been decided at that time. Until its demise in 1962, the new forward control C-Type would enjoy a revised edition of the S-Type cab scaled to suit the middle-weight chassis. For bus (and many commercial) body applications, a chassis cowl version was also produced.

Common to both forward and normal control models were the power units, but yet again changes were being made. The faithful 'Extra Duty' engine was re-designed and became the 214cu petrol engine, and it now produced 100bhp. The six-cylinder 300cu petrol engine introduced on the S-Type in 1950 received several modifications, not least of which was a new cylinder block. Also available was Bedford's new 300cu diesel engine, which had been designed to reduce dependence on outside manufacturers; in fact a new 200cu diesel was also being tested in some of the smaller D-Types in readiness for yet more development.

The Perkins 192cu P4 diesel was still a regular factory-fitted unit, but the Perkins R6 340cu engine was only being used for special applications. So it has to be said that the changes introduced with the C- and D- types were merely transitional, and it was obvious to many people that something new was just around the corner. This 'something' was the new TJ range, which burst on to the scene in 1958.

Top Left: *In a line-up that actually includes three D-Type vans, three A-Type vans (with Spurling bodies) and an OL lorry. Whilst we could not quite squeeze the entire fleet of the Kirklees Yarn Spinners from Bury into the space available for this page, this 1957 view shows just how popular the A- and D- types were with many businesses.*

Middle Left: *Back in the 1950s, Britain's nationalised coal mining industry was big business and central to the nation's economy. In the few short years since the National Coal Board had been formed, major steps had been taken in improving the Mines Rescue Service. Although this service had been formed by amalgamations of colliery-owners many years earlier, it was a cornerstone of the Labour Party manifesto, and within a very short period of time modern rescue equipment was being supplied to the brave miners who put their own lives at risk to help save their fellow workers. This D-Type personnel-carrier/fire-tender was allocated to the East Midlands Division of the NCB in the Mansfield area. Seen alongside a coal merchants' OWLE (a 5-ton long chassis built for civilian use under Ministry of War Transport licence), the D-Type pauses in a colliery yard on a rainy 13th June 1958.*

Bottom Left: *Complimentary with the D-Type chassis, were the C-Type middle-weight commercial models, which obviously falls outside the scope of this book. Yet for the sake of completeness, and as another prompt for our companion book* Bedford Buses of the 1950s & '60s, *I am taking the liberty of showing this C-Type 4-ton coach with the 'New Duple Vista' C29F body seen in the Cotswolds in 1959.*

In 1958 the millionth Bedford a (S-Type) was produced at Luton, which meant that it had taken 16 years to produce the first half-million Bedfords of which nearly a quarter of a million were built during the war years, but only 11-years to build the next half-million. Yet the speed of production was set to accelerate, and by the end of 1960 the daily aggregate would total 275, and that was 365 days a year.

The light-weight D-Type played a relatively small part in the Bedford success story, but it did play a part. It was a holding model that kept the aging A-type in production up to the eve of the 1960s, and kept the company at the forefront of the market until it could release its new models for the decade ahead - and what new models they were, for the TJ and TK series became the most successful of all British trucks. In the meantime the A-Type light-weights still did a remarkable job, and they were to be found in all forms, doing all kinds of work, not only in Britain, but all over the world.

One important relationship that developed with the D-Type was that between Bedford and the bodybuilders Hawson, and this became especially evident in the TJ series that followed, with Hawson offering a large variety of bodies on that chassis. One of the most popular of these would be the 'Three-way Access' van on the D-Type, and the 'Easy Access' van body on the C-Type. Both of these bodies, and several varieties of tipper truck were tested on the C- and D- types in 1957-8 as a prelude to what would be offered for the TJ.

THE TJ-SERIES 25-CWT TO 3-TON

The 'something round the corner' was unveiled at the 1958 Commercial Motor Show and it really stamped its mark on the light-to middle-weight commercial market. In many ways the new TJ range was really just a step on from the later D-Types. Mechanically they carried on the broad specifications of their predecessors, and when it came to styling the parentage was easily defined. Yet there were big differences between the TJs and the A-Type, notably in terms of driver comfort and convenience.

The most obvious thing was the new one-piece panoramic window that had been given to both styles of TJ cab, and also the most pronounced slope to the bonnet. The two cabs varied only in front-end detail, but these differences are an important visual method of identifying between the light-weight models and the rest of the range. The models under 4-tons had vertically slatted grills and very stylish front wings, these wings featured a modest, yet pronounced cowl above the headlamps which were affectionately known as 'eyebrows'. The sidelights were also a stylised feature of the wing, contained, as they were, at the outer end of a long pressing in the wing that ran forward from the wheel arches. All the light-weights also featured 16-inch wheels.

Top Left: *This smart collection of Hartley's five TJ2 diesel vans was highly representative of many company-owned fleets in the late 1950s and early 1960s. Before the advent of the Bedford TK, the* Commercial Motor *magazine said: 'This is the modern van design for the '60s and we reckon that big things will come out from the driver-friendly, economical new diesel models from Bedford.' As an aside, when this picture was taken in late 1958, this was perhaps the only sort of 'jam' you'd see on Britain's roads.*

The heavier models had a wing shape not dissimilar to the D-Type, and like the earlier models the radiator grill was made up from horizontal slatted bars. The big difference however, was the fact that the horizontal bars stretched right across the front of the truck, from headlamp to headlamp. Internally the cab was 'driver-friendly', noise was reduced to a minimum, and both the steering and the ride were much better. The three-seats made it a mini crew-cab as well!

Yet the parentage of the cab, through the Bedford TA- and TD-types was still clearly obvious, and if you trace it back, those cabs had their origins in the General Motors 'Advanced Design Cab', which had been first introduced on a Chevrolet truck in the spring of 1947. The new bonnet on the TJ series gave better close-range forward vision, and this gave the truck a more stylish appearance.

Top Left: *In a range of models that spanned the light to middleweight spectrum, the new TJ swept the board. The car-like appointments made them firm favourites with their drivers, and their economical purchase price and reasonable running costs made them a favourite of many operations. At the bottom end of the spectrum, the 25-cwt J1 is represented here by a dropside truck.*

Middle Left: *With the arrival of the TJ series, Bedford started to offer even more factory-built options, and this pick-up truck succeeded the 'approved' Walker pick-up that had been recommended by Bedford on the A- and D- type chassis cab. This particular model, pictured in February 1959, was used on the Trans-European Convoy which ran from south-west Portugal to northern Finland. Strangely, when the company came to use this picture in publicity material, the Bedford name and Vauxhall badge were masked out.*

Bottom Left: *It was not only the small Bedford commercials that were used by newspaper firms, for the TJ model became a firm favourite with both national and regional journals, especially the Hawson bodied van with its sliding doors. Yet a number of standard bonnet chassis cowls were supplied to builders like Vincent, Smiths, Toller and Jennings, for construction as newspaper vans with front sliding doors. This one (EYX 263C) was supplied to the Daily Express in 1965.*

Like the TA and TD, the TJ would lose its 'T' prefix and become better known as the J-Type, and it is generally noted that Bedford designed 11 models within the J-Type range. However, during the course of preparing this book, we came across a TJ specification list that Vauxhall produced prior to the launch of the range, and this shows 12 models in the spectrum. These were J1/169 (^{1}/2-ton), J1 (1^1/4-ton), J1/166 (1^3/4-ton), J2Short (3-ton), J2Long (3-ton), J3 (4-ton 161-inch), J4 (5-ton 167-inch), J4A (8-ton tractor), J5 short (6-ton), J-5 Long (6-ton), J6 Short (7-ton), J6 Long (7-ton).

Now don't ask me why they did not give the models a numeral that signified their tonnage (eg: J2 = 2-ton, J6 = 6-ton etc.), but for this reason the designation confuses some people.But what about that proposed J1/code 169, well that would eventually become the JO, of which we will discuss more later. Out of the models in the list, the only ones that really concern us here are the J1 standard and the J1 code 166 as these were the only TJ models under our limit of 3-tons.

The limit of 2^1/2-tons being the maximum weight for a 'light-commercial' was in fact initially set by the Ministry of Transport. Anything 2^1/2-tons or under was permitted to travel at 30mph, whilst over that weight they were plated at a maximum speed of 20mph. However, the primary allocation of 'weight-saving materials', for example certain steels and aluminium, was directed to aircraft production during the war and heavier steel or cast-iron was used in commercial vehicle production and thus the light models were forced to became heavier. The Ministry therefore relaxed the 2^1/2-tons limit back to 3-tons, and manufacturers like Bedford changed the designation.

Eventually the speed restriction was dropped altogether after Britain recovered from the effects of the petrol rationing occasioned by the advent of the Suez Crisis. The Minister of Transport who gave this freedom, Harold Watkins, was vehemently accused of creating a road hauliers' charter. When coupling this action with other events of the period, notably the Buchannan report on motorways, the Beeching report on railways, and the free open market caused by the progressive 'sell-off' of British Road Services to the private sector, the critics were probably correct. Yet, the Suez crisis did impact heavily on the British transport scene in more ways than one, and at Vauxhall it brought about those new diesel engines that they had primarily developed for the TJs.

Before World War II, there had been a long conversation between GMs supremo Alex Taub, and my former boss David (later Sir David) Brown, This had centred on tank transmissions, on which both Bedford and David Brown would be working together after hostilities broke out, but it also included discussions on dieselisation. The two agreed that the engineer to consult was Harry Ricardo, and both Taub and Brown met with the acknowledged genius in the field. Whether this was together or separate I do not know, but in both cases a plan was hatched to create a diesel power plant from a petrol unit. Brown had his Cropmaster diesel of 1949 hatched from a design modification suggested for the VAK1 engine before it went into production in 1938. Vauxhall did something similar, but again it was many years before the dream became a reality, the advent of war delaying all such dreams.

In fact, I gather that a 300cu diesel power unit had really been intended for the M- and O- types, but as these sold well enough throughout the war years with petrol engines, there was no real need for a factory-fitted diesel. But it was that next conflict, the Suez Crisis that really brought the Bedford-Ricardo diesel out of mothballs. The need for fuel economy became a national concern, and diesel engines were viewed as being highly important. Yet not only was the 300cu development going on for the heavier commercial chassis, but also a 200cu diesel was being developed for the light- middle-weight models. It was these units, coupled with the highly successful petrol engines that would be so important in the new TJs.

Top Right: *This is a basic chassis-cab model, probably a 25-cwt version from the mid-1960s, which really doesn't look a lot different from the A- or D- types, especially when viewed from this angle.*

Middle Right: *The second variant on the TJ series is what was called the Easy-Access cab, which in turn came from the American 'walk-thru' concept.*

Bottom Right: *This normal model TJ chassis-cab has been built with a 'chariot' back and fitted with a crane for recovery work. This was in the days before recovery services were offered by the big motoring operations and when breakdown work was passed on to local garages. Here a TJ1 working for Blue Star Garages, Newport Pagnell Motorway Services, rescues a battered M-series Morris 10, whilst a Commer van is the only other vehicle on the motorway.*

Top Left: *Presenting something of a strain on the TJ1 chassis, this armoured car belonging to Securicor Ltd. (831 DLC) really looks back-end heavy. Look at the length of the overhang beyond the rear axle, then just imagine this full of gold bullion!!!!!!!!!!!!!!!!!!!*

Middle Left: *Looking much more like your every day van, and clearly demonstrating the point made earlier, just look at how this Hawson-bodied 'Easy-Access' semi-forward control TJ1 is ready for work. No front passenger seat means that a small step takes the driver down to door level, and another step puts him (or her) on the ground. 'Easy Access' by name, easy access by nature, and just the thing when you were hopping in and out of the cab with boxes or parcels all day long. Apart from loading through the rear doors at the depot in the morning, and getting out of the cab at night, the bulk of the driver's movement could have been made from the nearside door straight on to the pavement for the customer's door.*

Bottom Left: *Whilst outside the scope of this book, but emphasising the point, here we have UAR 716F a 1967 TJ3L (3-tonner), which had a gross vehicle weight of 7-tons. It too features the Hawson Easy Access body, and was employed by British Railways as fleet number 4VE2716F on the Midland Region's Rail Freight Sundry Traffic service. Along with the Commer Walk-Thru, BR found the TJ a perfect delivery vehicle for multi-drop and collection work. The entire story about British Railway road vehicles is told in yet another* **Nostalgia Road** *book for those who are interested.*

Given this development of cab, chassis and power units, the TJ was sure to be a success. It outlasted Bedford and passed into the range of models produced by AWD and after them it was built by Marshalls to special order (mainly export). In Britain it served for over three decades in almost every role imaginable, including tractor unit, 4x4 and tipper, but as a light commercial it played a remarkable role, filling the gap between the CA (later CF) range and heavy models. As a light truck (tipper, pick-up, platform and dropside) it had many applications, and it enjoyed much success as a normal control delivery van.

More importantly, as a semi-forward control chassis cowl unit, it also overcame a very serious threat to Bedford, from their rivals Commer. This Rootes Group firm were enjoying considerable success with their BF20 and BF30 vans, and later the 1¹/₂- to 2-ton Walk-Thru models, and were also taking markets that the CA was failing to hold, like for example, the new 'soft ice cream' vans, with their associated ice cream plants and mobile generators, or the big multi-drop delivery vans. But the semi-forward control TJ1 did all that the Commers did, and more. With the Hawson Easy Access cab, wide sliding doors allowed 'step in' access which was ideal for delivery work; roundsmen (whether they were carrying bread, parcels or other multi-drop consignments) just loved them. Some TJ vans can be seen with sliding doors, but these were generally built on chassis-cowls, whilst the standard chassis-cab generally had front-hinged doors - there again, I have found at least one picture showing a laundry van with rear-hinged (suicide) doors.

THE JO-TYPE 10-CWT

Above: *The super fast JO, with a middle-weight TK truck beyond.*

Living in Appleby-in-Westmorland, home to the famous Appleby Horse Fair, I could not ignore one of the fastest ever light pick-up trucks ever built by Bedford for the simple reason that this truck was well-loved by the Gypsy community. A figure of just 6,000 were sanctioned (in a number of separate build lots), but it seems likely that just under 5,300 were built in total between 1960 and 1965.

The little-known JO is often confused with its bigger brother the TJ, as it employed the cab of the larger truck, but it also used parts from the CA and the Cresta/Velox car. Indeed it used so many parts from existing Vauxhall-Bedford models, that about only a dozen new components were needed for this new truck. However, one important new feature was the all-new light truck chassis. It had pressed steel channel section with five cross-members and was put together by the cold-rivetting technique. It employed virtually the same suspension as the J1 although it had slightly longer springs. The wheels came from the early CA, but it used 6.70 x 15.6 6-ply Firestone car tyres. At the heart of it all was the 2651cc 104hp engine employed on the PA Velox/Cresta models. A 3-speed gearbox, similar in design to the CA but having the ratios of the PA was employed, and the CA's column change gear lever fitted in the cab.

The result was a fast truck that could pull away from a set of traffic lights and leave even powerful saloon cars standing. I recall travelling in one down the M1 in the late 1960s, and it had the speedo arm pressed hard against the stop peg just beyond the 90mph mark. I suppose we were doing around 100mph as we shot down the hill heading away from Barnsley to a rush job in Worksop.

It was in essence a foreman's or owner's truck that could rapidly sprint from one site or job to the next, but its 10-cwt payload was woefully inadequate and many businesses found it more practical to purchase the J1 or even the J2. To prolong its life, in November 1964 it was decided to use the new 3,300cc engine that was to be fitted to the new PC Cresta then on road test. Unfortunately, the sales of the JO had fallen away to a very low level, and the model was dropped from the Bedford range in August 1965 before all the sanctioned-build figures were reached. Many people say the JO was a failure, but in reality it was a truck ahead of its time. It was certainly well-liked in many quarters, especially in the export market. The fact that it did not have massive development costs probably counted against it, and if Vauxhall had spent much more on its creation, they may have been tempted to persevere with it longer than they did.

THE HA SERIES 6-CWT & 8-CWT

Throughout the history of Bedford commercial vehicles, you can trace a progressive development programme, for only in 1939 did we see a complete range of new models being introduced right across the board. For the rest of the time the company was quite content to do 'staged' development, attending first to one target audience, whilst considering the next. As a result, a new range would be developed and tested, and whilst it was being launched the company would be developing the next range. This meant that, during a given period of time all the public activity might be centred on a particular brand of heavy commercial, whilst the actual secret development work would have been going on with a new light-weight model. Whilst this was generally the case, the only exception was with the development of the HA van, which came about because this was the company's first car-derived lightweight Bedford van since the HC.

Yet, since the re-vamp of the CA in 1959, when the capacity went up to 15-cwt, the lighter end of its market had been slowly eroding away. The opposition was now becoming very fierce, with the Austin A35 and the Morris 1000 from BMC, Ford's 300E and the small Commers. By the early 1960s a surprising competitor came in the shape of the Renault Fourgon (later known as the 4L), but most makers were seeing the benefits of producing a car-derived van.

Three really outstanding examples of this are seen in the derivatives of the Ford Anglia 105E/123E, the BMC Mini and the Hillman Imp. From these three makers came a range of superb and highly practical light commercials, and between them they sliced away quite a large chunk of the CA's market. Of these, the Hillman was the least successful, and it really posed little worry to Vauxhall, but the other two - especially the Ford 307E was a major threat and despite only having a 997cc four-cylinder ohv engine, its four-speed gearbox was a distinct improvement on the three-speed 300E vans.

40

Top Left: *In a pre-model release publicity photograph, a prototype 8-cwt HA is pictured with the works trade plate 147 ENM. In the accompanying material, the press release date 21st August 1964 read, 'While inheriting all the driver comfort, ease of handling and performance of the new Vauxhall Viva, the new Bedford 6-cwt and 8-cwt vans have been designed and developed as 100% commercial vehicles right from the start. The Viva front end harmonises completely with a neat and smoothly styled body to make a really smart van of 70 cubic feet capacity.'*

Top Right: *Either someone took the above HA back into the works and altered its configuration, or someone swapped the registration plate 147 ENM on to a red 6-cwt van. This was the economy model, and like the picture shown above it was taken in June 1964.*

Bottom Right: *Seen from ground level, and thus showing quite a bit of the HA's underside, this 6-cwt van was used in publicity material at the end of 1966, after being filmed in June that year.*

Therefore, by the time Vauxhall had got its new light commercial into the market place, it had already lost considerable ground, and sales of the CA also suffered as a result. For many applications, especially newspapers, small shops, the construction industry 'secondary trades' (plumbers, joiners, electricians etc.), the Ford 307E 'Anglia' van was ideal. Even the BMC Mini, offered with both Austin and Morris badges, was a very practical van, and the pick-up version also played a very useful role. Never being a small person I had a profound dislike of the Mini commercials, but I actually learned to drive in a 1965 Renault (GCX 712C), and my first car was an Austin A35 estate car (3761 U)!

Yet, despite the success of their new Mini, the two other light commercials from BMC, the Austin A35 and the Morris 1000, were both dated and more than a little staid. Like the CA they tended to suffer from a bulbous appearance, whereas 1960s styling was definitely disposed towards more angular lines. Therefore, having let Ford get away from them with the 307E, it seems fairly obvious that Vauxhall were aiming their new car-derived van at two markets. First of all their main desire was to retain the loyalty of the former CA owners, and therefore prevent competitors making an incursion into their market.

Secondly, there was also perceived to be something of a chance to take something away from BMC, as both the 1000 and the A35 were being considered as being a bit under-powered for the faster road speeds that were becoming necessary in the 1960s. It was into this background that the HA van was born under Alex Williamson the Commercial Vehicle Engineer. Reporting to John Alden, Williamson, and his team were engaged in a variety of projects in the early 1960s. His 'B Team' were given the job of starting the projects, whilst the 'C Team' took over and saw the job through to completion.The new Bedford light commercial came under this arrangement, and with the basis of a new car design already well advanced, the van derivative was not too complicated. In the end it was a design that would span over 20 years, as the very last HAs were produced in 1985.

Top Left: *In a picture taken on the Brache Estate at Luton, with the Vauxhall plant in the background, we see the rear aspect of the HA van. The wide-opening rear doors made this a popular little van, and it was one that had very little major opposition at the time, for with the exception of the Ford Thames 307E (derived from the Anglia saloon), all its major competitors were rather dated.*

Middle Left: *With a backdrop of one TK tractor unit and no less than four Constellation aircraft, an 8-cwt Bedford HAD van is seen at Luton Airport in September 1964. This was a setting for many of Vauxhall's publicity pictures in the 1950s and 1960s, and some years before Lorraine Chase and Easy-jet brought the airport other kinds of publicity.*

Bottom Left: *As mentioned before, Bedford (and Vauxhall cars come to that) had enjoyed a long association with Martin Walter from Folkestone. This enterprising coachbuilders had modified a variety of cars and light commercials, with perhaps the Dormobile being the most famous. As we will discuss shortly, they carried on this connection with the HA, but one of their early offerings was a rather surprising, yet nevertheless very functional high-top HA van. By replacing the roof with a glass-fibre unit, and adding a hinged top tail-gate, most of the basic body shell and the rear doors were retained. Complete with a stylish female model, this feature is well shown in this 1965 picture.*

Now, whilst this is not a book about cars, I have no real option but to look at the history of the HA saloon, and to do this I am quoting directly from the book *Vauxhall Cars 1945 - 1964*, which we produced for Vauxhall Heritage Services, it reads:-

The need for a small saloon was becoming essential to the Vauxhall range, at a time when the working classes were changing from public transport to private car ownership. Essentially the motorcycle combination had proved to be the entry point for the family market, but the great success of the Morris 1000, Austin A30/A35, the small Rootes Group cars and Ford's Anglia/ Popular/ Prefect 100E and the Anglia 105E had shown that here was a market that really could not be ignored by Vauxhall. The main problem was that Luton was already being worked to capacity, and the output on the larger cars showed no sign of diminishing. In 1955 the Bedford truck production had to be moved to a new plant at Dunstable, and this plant was also working to capacity as the millionth Bedford was produced in 1958. The following year Luton turned out the 2-millionth Vauxhall, and there was literally no capacity for a small car.

To address the problem of capacity, and given the incentive of selective financial assistance, the company announced that it was to open a new plant at Hooton, near Ellesmere Port on the south side of the River Mersey. Located on the site of a former RAF base, the site offered good communications by road, rail and sea, and of course it was also in one of the Economic Development Areas.

The Vauxhall Directors considered many other alternatives, but the Cheshire site won out, and it was decided that it would be the base for the manufacture of the new 'H Concept' car. Construction work began in August 1960, and the first Viva rolled off the specially-built Ellesmere Port plant in August 1964. However, the success of the small BMC and Ford saloons (especially the Mini), prompted Vauxhall to commence the production of some Viva saloons at Luton in September 1963, just in time for the forthcoming Motor Show.

Another essential requirement for the new saloon, was the potential to develop into car-derived commercial vehicles. Light vans, pick-up trucks and small estate cars were all planned around the 1057cc four-cylinder engine. This strong little engine had a large bore and a short stroke, a down-draught single Solex carburettor, and produced 44bhp giving a top speed of around 80mph. Transmission was by an all synchromesh four-speed gearbox, using a short floor-mounted gear stick. This gave much faster changes through the gears, and thus made it ideal for new drivers!

The resulting HA van was a delight to drive, it was light in weight, had good petrol economy, a powerful 1057cc engine, and was very easy to drive. The one big fault I found was that the rear axle always seemed a bit on the light side, but this would be remedied when the 10-cwt HAV van was introduced with a sturdier back end.

Top Right: *A number of other modifications were undertaken by Vauxhall, as the little HA soon became a light-weight 'Jack of all trades' to complement its big brothers the CA and the TJ. Yet not all modifications were tried out in the flesh, at least initially, and when someone suggested making a pick-up version the Styling Department decided to make a mock-up. Blacking out the top of a standard HAD van on this photograph, and drawing in a pick-up body, the finished result was visualised. The pick-up was eventually an approved variation, yet someone hadn't done their job right. Look at the 'cab' roof in this picture, and you will see that the end of a pair of ladders appear on the roof, what a fundamental blunder!*

Middle Right: *Despite the odd mistake or two along the way, the HA went on to enjoy a long and successful life, and some of these worked in pretty exciting surroundings. Here a 1975 HA is seen at work with a Chevette and a TK box van in the service of Hesketh Racing. The Formula One car alongside is a Hesketh 308, which was driven by James Hunt who later won the world championships.*

Bottom Right: *In the absence of anywhere else to logically place this picture, we show the HB Viva van. Whilst the HA saloon and estate were superseded by the HB in 1966, the boxy HA went on in the commercial field for many years. Yet, in an estate car-derived model, the HB van was available as a 'special conversion' as seen in this December 1967 view. Yet Vauxhall's view must have been, 'if it ain't broke, don't fix it', and the HA van was never even threatened by the much more superior HB.*

Top Left: *This trio of pictures shows the Bedford Beagle, which was really an estate car version of the HA saloon, yet based on the van, Therefore, it was neither fish nor fowl in some ways, and whilst being a passenger carrying model, it was badged as a Bedford. As many people purchased them to serve the dual functions of family use and commercial work. This selection of pictures shows off the Bedford Beagle to good effect. First of all, this publicity picture shows the 1057cc engined Beagle parked outside John Bright's hardware and ironmongery store in Kempston, Bedfordshire - a town more famous for its 'Fletton' bricks than plastic laundry baskets.*

Middle Left: *The next port of call was the Swan Inn, but look through the windows into the load space at the back, the laundry baskets have transformed into a set of large suitcases.*

Bottom Left: *This February 1965 picture, although contrived looks a little more realistic, as it shows the Martin Walter conversion in a little more detail, including the driver's controls and the opening centre section in the rear window.*

The four-speed gear box, with its highly sensible floor-change gear lever was an instantaneous hit, especially with those drivers changing down from the CA. Also getting good reviews was the rack and pinion steering, which made the HA van very easy to steer. In fact, if anything the HA was too light on the steering, and this affected road holding, especially when running empty and driving in bad conditions. Kindness prevents me from mentioning the name of a very good friend who managed to slide one of these HAs down Knowle Lane at Meltham in 1971. He went all the way from the top of the David Brown Tractors test road down to the offices one January morning - approximately a quarter of a mile, sideways.

Nevertheless, handling problems apart, the HA van was a superbly economical light commercial and it sold well into many large fleets, notably the regional gas companies, the electricity boards, water authorities, British Railways and Post Office Telephones. Bedford had hoped that its new van would also oust the Morris 1000 from the Royal Mail fleet, but this narrowly failed to come about.

The HA was also modified for a number of special applications, including a rather stylish 'high top', which Martin Walter designed primarily for the garment trade. A good number of these were also sold to laundry companies, whilst several local authorities employed them in their 'Park & Gardens' departments. A milk float version was offered, and Martin Walter also made a camper van version, on which we will hear more later! A pick up version of the HA was also produced, and a unique picture in this chapter shows the very 'first pick-up'!

Firms like Morrisons, Cummins and Archibald Scott converted them to ice cream vans and burger bars. One of the oddest conversions to the HA was the offering by Cummins of Crewe, who produced the 'Batman' mobile. This featured a very high extension to the body, and the front of this had a pair of windows shaped like 'bat eyes', whilst the fibre-glass roof came complete with tail fins and rocket jet!

Although we have already discussed the next derivative of the HA van in the book, *Vauxhall Cars 1945-1964*, The Bedford Beagle also belongs in this book as well. This car-cum-commercial was a nice marriage of resources to meet the needs of both small businesses and commercial traveller's in the 1960s. In essence, the Bedford Beagle could serve as a commercial vehicle during the day, and yet convert into a small family saloon for evenings and weekends. It was a concept really developed by Morris with their 1000 Traveller, and to a lesser extent by the Austin A35 Countryman and the Hillman Husky, but it was a market that the boxy little HA van could readily be adapted to by the application of only a few minor factory line changes. The HA van was thus suited for a wide number of applications, both business and pleasure, and sometimes a mixture of both. Mechanically it was very little different to the saloon, but bodily there were several obvious differences. One major body difference was the doors on the van, which Alden considered needed to be larger than those used on the car.

The 6-cwt (HAE) and 8-cwt (HAD) were really the start of the matter, and as mentioned earlier a 10-cwt van (HAV) was added in 1972, but the boxy shape of the commercial considerably outlasted the HA saloon. It was superseded by the very stylish HB Viva in 1966, and although Vauxhall seriously considered changing the van style as well, the 'Coke-bottle' styling of the saloon did not readily suit a commercial vehicle. A van version of the estate was produced, but it was never intended to replace the HA van, which remained in regular production until 1983 and a few 'specials' were being turned out as late as 1985.

Top Right: *For a variety of reasons, I have tried to stay away from the subject of mobile caravans or caravanettes in this book, for the simple reason they were not really commercial vehicles. Yet as they were derived from them, I let myself go with the HA to let one selection of pictures illustrate how commercial vehicles could be adapted for more pleasurable pursuits. All three images show the Martin Walter caravanette, the first one being the departure in BNS 157F. The mobile home may have included everything you needed, including a kitchen sink, but obviously hubby forgot the kettle.*

Middle Right: *When you got to your destination, as the couple in OKO 215G had obviously done in 1969, it was time to set up camp. Up went the roof to provide extra headroom, and down went the rear tailgate, which was bottom hinged to allow a fabric extension at the back.*

Bottom Right: *And with all that done, so to bed. Comfortable and snug, and safe from the rigors of the weather - well almost. My only trip in a 'camper' proved to be somewhat different! In October 1969, whilst on a trip to Blackpool Illuminations with my parents and my girlfriend Larraine, I came round the back of the camper only to be met with a bowl of water being thrown out of the van by Larraine. I was soaked to the skin! Still, I must have forgiven her, as we got married in July 1971, and we are celebrating our 30th anniversary the week this book is released, and with all my love I dedicate it to her.*

The TK Lightweight Series 30-cwt To 2-Ton

There is no doubt in my mind, that the smartest truck to emerge in the 1960s was the Bedford TK. Whilst its 'cab-ahead-of-engine' concept would be copied by many manufacturers in due course, this new offering from Bedford was so far ahead of its time as to describe the impact it had when it was released at the Commercial Motor Show in 1960. The cab itself was not only quiet (from having the engine tucked away behind), but it was driver friendly in many other ways too. The boxy, flat-front concept would be successfully copied in the 'ergonomic' cabs fitted to Leyland, Albion and AEC trucks, but it was Bedford who led the pace with the TK. Like the new range of bus chassis that would soon follow (the VAS and VAL), the TK employed 16-inch wheels to give a low loading height, and was a complete contrast with the bulbous-fronted, high platform height of the S-Type and R-Type that had preceded it.

The first of the 12 new forward-control TK models rolled off the Dunstable assembly line on 4th August 1960, to provide a range of models in the 3-ton to 12-ton bracket. There was a choice of either petrol or diesel engine, and either a four- or five- speed gearbox.

But, hold on for a moment, you may ask; 'Isn't this a book about light commercials?' Obviously the answer has to be yes, but it may well surprise some to know that although the initial TK range was 3-tons or above, there would eventually be a range of lightweight models as well.

Whilst the needs of the businesses or haulage companies were quite adequately catered for by the range of the TJ models, it soon became quite obvious that the success of the driver-friendly forward control cab was proving to be something of a dilemma for the sales team. As the bigger models became more and more popular with drivers, it was evident that a model in the 30-cwt to 2-ton category would be needed if Bedford were to supply the whole range.

Top Left: *About the time I was getting up the nerve to propose to my girlfriend Larraine, I was also being interviewed for a job with the David Brown Corporation as a Commercial Apprentice. Now Sir David Brown, the owner of David Brown Tractors, Vosper Thornycroft and Aston Martin, had a long relationship with Vauxhall Motors that stemmed back to the war years. In fact Brown's had done a lot of work on tank transmissions, and Dr. E. (Ted) Merritt who had been at Luton went to work for Brown at Meltham Mills. He knew my father quite well, and I can just remember the great engineer as a child. Now around this time one of Vauxhall's directors was in need of a new tractor or two (I can't say what for), and Brown needed some better transport for his work force. As a result a couple of OWB chassis were swapped for a pair of VAK1C Cropmaster tractors, and everyone was happy. Yet it was just one of a number of deals that took place over the years, and it was not uncommon for Bedford or Vauxhall vehicles to appear in DB publicity shots, nor for DB products to appear in Vauxhall pictures. To prove the point, and in a rather long-winded way of showing a 2-ton TKB tipper, we see a David Brown 990 Selectamatic at work in Devon. It is registered in 1965, but as it is an early 'white model' it can only have been put on the road in the period 15th October - 31st December. Oh, and in case you'd thought I'd forgot about the 1967-registered lorry, it belonged to Longdon's of Topsham and features a Hawson tipping body.*

Top Right: *When it was felt that the normal control TJ models were not filling all the needs in the 30-cwt to 2-ton market, it was decided to build a lighter TK. Design work seems to have been commenced in 1963, but the new models were not introduced until 1965 when payloads of 30-cwt and 2-ton were announced alongside a modified 3-tonner and a new 111/2-ton tipper. This was really the first stage in a major development of the forward control models, for in 1966 the larger KM range was launched to span the 14-ton to 16-ton bracket. But back to the smaller TKs, and in June 1965 we see a 30-cwt light van with a foreign number plate (B33 CXD).*

Middle Right: *Now here is an interesting shot, as it shows a modified TK chassis, with twin rear wheels and a small Walker van body. It was obviously used to promote the new lightweight TKs, but instructions on the back of the print state 'show only single rear wheels - 6-stud'. The picture was taken on 19th March, but it was not for release until a given date - though I've no idea what that date actually was!*

Bottom Right: *And finally, just by way of contrast, I couldn't leave the subject without showing the biggest unit in the range, the articulated tractor. At 12-tons it has no real place in this book, but in my defence I use this picture as it shows other light commercials. Yet who can deny that this picture of a TK car transporter has a rightful place in this book? Seen on 27th March 1961, the Dealers Deliveries Ltd. TK carries an F-Type Victor, PA Velox, two CA chassis-cowls, and a standard CA van - well standard in some ways, but very special in others for this was the 200,000th Bedford van to be built.*

THE CF SERIES 14-CWT TO 35-CWT

Having almost reached the end of this book, it will be evident that, throughout the course of my narrative, I have not gone heavily into the technical details of the models I have been discussing. The simple reasoning behind this is three-fold. Firstly, this series of books is merely intended as an overview of the history and development of the Bedford range of vehicles. Secondly, the books are intended to place this development into a social and historical context, and show how the development had an inter-relation with a number of other events simultaneously going on. Thirdly, a lack of space has precluded our going into the depth we would have really liked to use to explain the subject. Therefore, it is our intention that, with the continuing support of Vauxhall Motors and the Vauxhall Heritage Service, we will return to look at a number of these models in-depth and cover each within their own exclusive volume.

I hope that this will encourage readers to come forward with contributions for these books, the first of which will be on the CA. Experiences, anecdotal information and photographs would all be greatly appreciated, as in these books we will try and continue the theme of social and practical application, along with more specialist technical data. That said, we must also look at the extraneous events within the British motor industry in general, for the development within one maker's range of cars, vans or trucks certainly influenced the development in their competitors. And nowhere was the fact more clearly seen than in the new Bedford CF.

The CAs replacement hit the roads in 1969, but what came out in the CF was, in many ways a knee jerk reaction to the marketing of Ford's must successful commercial vehicle to date - the new Transit. In many ways the success of the CA was also the downfall of the CF, for had Vauxhall revolutionised the appearance of the CA in the mid-1960s, then the Transit's impact may have been significantly less.

Top Left: *Whilst Bedford had enjoyed 13 years of unrivalled prominence with the CA van, Ford's V project under the control of Vernon Smith had been launched simultaneously in Britain (as the Transit), and Germany (as the Taunus). The arrival of an exciting new van from GM's arch rivals prompted styling changes to the Bedford 15-cwt models, but what resulted was never quite as exciting. This May 1969 shot shows one of the prototype 14-cwt CFs on the company's test ground at Chaul End.*

Top Right: *An earlier prototype based on a CAL, seen at Chaul End on 3rd July 1968 shows a three-way loading CF on a left-hand drive version of the 15-cwt model.*

Middle Right: *Yet a further prototype, this time a 35-cwt twin rear wheel chassis cab, which was seen as being the ideal version for bodying as 'heavy load carriers'. Included in the applications planned for this chassis were ambulances, but when a decision was taken on buying a large batch of chassis for ambulance bodies, the NHS opted for single rear wheels instead. In the fullness of time it was found that this was a potentially fatal error, as wheels started dropping off ambulances and up in County Durham some particularly serious incidents occurred, although fortunately no-one was ever injured.*

Bottom Right: *Although suffering from motion blur on the two workers in the foreground, this picture has to be included as it shows the first of the CF vans going through the primer surface sprayer booths in F and G Blocks at Dunstable.*

During the 1950s Ford had nothing to touch the CA, and nor did BMC or Rootes if you really think about it, for economy and versatility were the watchword of the Vauxhall product. However, Ford were very conscious about this, and envious of the great success that Bedford was enjoying in the cheaper end of the commercial vehicle market, they decided to do something about it. The assault came first in the middle-weight range, and with the new Thames Trader the Dunstable products were given a run for their money. Vauxhall were so concerned about this that they went to a lot of trouble to fight off the competition.

One almost churlish piece of evidence I have discovered is a picture of a Vauxhall saloon running through central London, closely followed by a Thames truck going about its lawful business. However, to ensure that the Ford product did not get any free publicity at the expense of Bedford, when the Vauxhall picture was reproduced for publication, the front end of the Thames Trader was 'artistically re-touched' to make it appear to be something else.

Yet in the light commercial field Bedford felt they had really no major concerns, as the CA really did fill a massive portion of the market. However, about the time that Bedford were making cosmetic changes to the MkII CA, Ford were instituting their V programme. This dated back to 1961 and was to be headed by Vernon Smith, who had been instructed to come up with a design to replace the rather staid offerings that Ford were producing in Britain at that time.

Top Left: *The initial range of CF models is well illustrated in this selection of pictures from the summer of 1969, commencing first of all with the 14-cwt chassis-cab version which carries a pick-up body. The styling on this once again has a distinct Stateside feel about it, and there is little wonder that the United States Air Force purchased quite a few of these pick-ups (left-hand drive of course) for use in Europe.*

Middle Left: *Ignoring the advice given by a number of designers against using the 22-cwt as an emergency ambulance body, was to prove a costly mistake for all the parties involved! Yet as a light ambulance - one mainly used for sitting cases or outpatient transport - the 18-cwt chassis was ideal. Here we see a modified CF Deluxe used as a mixed emergency/transport unit, although I can find no record of the firm carrying out this conversion, it may well have been by Hanlon in Northern Ireland.*

Bottom Left: *Next we see a 22-cwt chassis-cab finished with a box van body produced by Marshall's of Cambridge. The picture dates from 4th September 1969, but reproduction was prohibited until 31st October that year.*

As readers will appreciate, the reality of the V Project was the new Transit van (also with chassis-cab and chassis-cowl versions), which came out in 1965. Immediately it impacted on the sales of the CA, for this was already a 13-year old design by that time. Yes, there had been face-lifts and substantial improvements, but it was still a 13-year old concept, and some things can go on for too long. What is more, the long-running success of the CA had stilted the birth of so many other Bedford projects, namely the CB, CD and CE, each of which had been taken through the design process but never put into full production. One of these was for a full forward control version of the CA, but this had been dropped when Ford launched its Thames Trader 400E van and Bedford had decided not to be seen to be following Ford. But that is exactly what it would be forced to do with the CF.

Now it will be evident that I am a fan of the CA, and equally evident that I think that the CF was not all that special. But the reality is that Vauxhall were caught napping or being too complacent, and Ford romped away with their new success. As I have spent many hours looking through the official records of both Bedford and Ford, I do have a little insight into the matter, perhaps uniquely so.

I know that within weeks of the Transit's launch, models had been bought by Bedford, and in common with many automotive firms of that time, Vauxhall made a very thorough study of the Transit. What they saw evidently alarmed them, for here was the real replacement for the CA, and if it was not being made by Bedford, it was also to be seen as a very serious threat. The answer was to launch a competing, preferably superior model, but there was nothing really special in the design stages, and Bedford were forced to look at an American concept, the panel van, as its answer to the Transit. What came out in 1969 was not dissimilar to the Transit, and although the two were close competitors, the new offering should have revolutionised the market.

The CF absorbed the inclined four-cylinder petrol engines from the 1967 FD Victor (1599cc and 1957cc), but two Perkins diesel engines were factory-fitted options. There were two wheel bases for the new CF, these being the short version at 106-inches (2.7m) and the long version at 126-inches (3.2m). Mind you, it may be something of a misnomer to call the smaller of the two CFs a short wheelbase model, as it was some 4-inches (10cm) longer than the old CAL. As a result of these extensions in length the standard swb van now had a carrying capacity of 185 cubic feet, whilst the lwb model had 252 cubic feet.

As noted above there was a variety of carrying capacities, and the swb model had three sizes 14-cwt, 18-cwt and 22-cwt, whilst the lwb came in 25-cwt and 35-cwt. Of these the 14-cwt and the 18-cwt used the Vauxhall 1599cc petrol engine or the Perkins 4.108 diesel, whilst the 22-cwt swb, 25-cwt and 35-cwt had the 1957cc petrol or the new Perkins 4.154 diesel. The petrol engines were quite high-revving at first, and at 5,500rpm they developed 64bhp and 75bhp respectively. The slower smooth pulling speed of the CA was lost, and many drivers used to carrying heavy loads found that the engines were not well suited to their trade, especially builders and the like. Others complained of high noise levels. But, once the CF was rolling, it was a very lively vehicle despite the sizeable load space it carried. The smaller engined versions could have either a three- or four-speed gearbox, but the larger engines could only have the four-speed box.

By the time the CF was finally discontinued, it had gained many adherents, but it never made up all the ground lost to the Transit. There are those who truly loved the CF, and I can understand why, but they were never really as innovative as the CA had been. Ford had seen a gap and capitalised on it, and whilst there wasn't a lot to choose between the Transit and the CF in the long run, it always seemed to me that Bedford were in fact playing 'catch-up'! Moreover the Transit is still with us (after more metamorphoses than those other 1960s creations, Doctor Who and James Bond), whereas the Bedford CF is sadly history!

Top Right: *Clad with another Marshall body, this time a 'small pantechnicon' we see the biggest of the new CF range, the 35-cwt Deluxe model. As yet the body has to receive its first coat of paint, and the weld detail is clearly evident.*

Middle Right: *Once again the firm of Martin Walter were to be deeply involved with the new CF, and this 7th July 1969 picture shows their new Dormobile conversion from an 18-cwt van. The publicity view is taken at Folkestone, with the French ferry* Cote D'Azur *and a British Railways ferry in the docks beyond.*

Bottom Right: *And finally, we must not forget Smith's Delivery Vehicles, makers of mobile shops, ice cream vans, milk floats and many other special bodies. They too made much use of the new CF and here we see their 'new style' body designed for the 1970s. As an ice cream van, it was called the Cornette '70, and it first made an appearance in or around 1967 or 1968 on the CAL. This particular CF delivery van was photographed on 4th September 1969.*

ACKNOWLEDGEMENTS

This book has very much been a labour of love, and also a trip back to my youth when Bedford light commercials were everywhere. The truth of that advertising slogan will be impressed upon my memory for a very long time, as will the friendliness of the public relations department of Vauxhall Motors. It will never cease to amaze me how gullible they were in responding to all those 'school work' projects I wrote to them about, and to which they would send (invariably by return mail) a mass of information and photographs.

If I had really done so much school work my parents and teachers would have been amazed. Probably the Vauxhall staff knew this and were just being kind, but they were a complete contrast to Ford, BMC and Commer, who rarely (if ever) answered my requests, even when they were genuine school projects. Travelling to school on Bedford SBs, and later having a part time job, in which I rode around in both CA vans and TK trucks, left me with a real passion for these wonderful machines.   **AE**

Above: *And, last but by no means least, that 200,000th Bedford van! This 'milestone' was a 15-cwt CA, and it is seen here as it rolled off the Dunstable assembly line in March 1961 much to the delight of all concerned. I wonder what became of it?*

I must now offer my sincere thanks to all those who have helped me with this project, and offer grateful appreciation to the following for their support:

Ron Atkins,	Mike Berry,	Robert Berry,
Peter Blincow,	Terry Calvert,	Ray Cooper,
Steve & Mandy Daniels,	Nigel Griggs	Stuart Harris,
Barry Harvey,	Richard Haughey,	David Hine,
Ryland James,	John Rawlings,	Dennis Sherer,
Peter Stone,	Peter Relph,	Ron Robinson,

But above all I must say a very big thank you to the team at Trans-Pennine, and their sub-contractors Barnabus Design and Kent Valley Colour Printers, who pulled out all the stops in order to have this book ready for its launch at the 2001 VBOA Gathering at Billing.